Salads

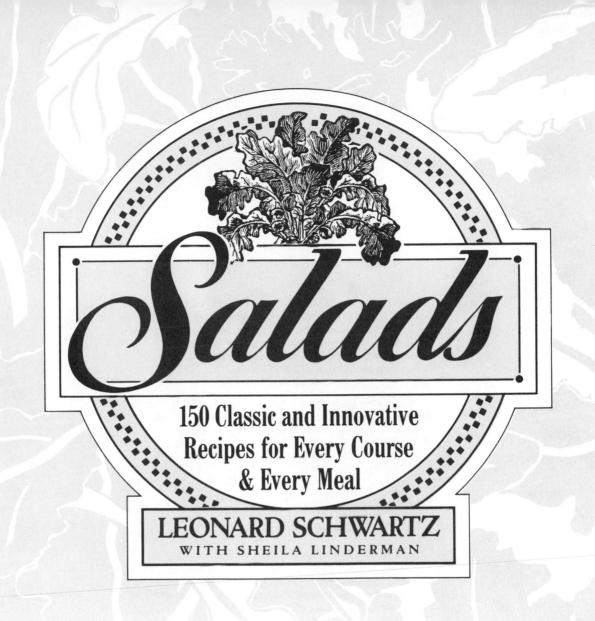

Salads

150 Classic and Innovative Recipes for Every Course & Every Meal

LEONARD SCHWARTZ

WITH SHEILA LINDERMAN

HarperCollins*Publishers*

HarperCollins books may be purchased for educational, business, or sales promotional use. For information, please call or write: Special Markets Department, HarperCollins Publishers, Inc., 10 East 53rd Street, New York, NY 10022. Telephone: (212) 207-7528; Fax: (212) 207-7222.

FIRST EDITION

DESIGNED BY JOEL AVIROM

Illustrations by Jim Cozza

Library of Congress Cataloging-in-Publication Data
Schwartz, Leonard, 1948–
Salads: 150 classic and innovative recipes for every course and every meal/ Leonard Schwartz.—lst ed.
p.   c.m.
Includes index.
ISBN 0-06-016239-2 (hardcover)
1. Salads.   I. Linderman, Sheila.   II. Title.
TX740.S326   1992
641.8'3—dc20   91-50446

92 93 94 95 96   DT/RRD   10 9 8 7 6 5 4 3 2 1

For my father, Morris Schwartz,
and for my wife and son,
Diane and Elliot Schwartz

CONTENTS

ACKNOWLEDGMENTS

I would like first to offer a thank-you to my colleagues, former and present, who have provided inspiration, ideas, and energy (not to mention good fun): Jere Anderson, who is so very much missed, Jose Cabrera, John Gress, Michael Novotney, Michael Rosen, Andrea Schaeffer, Robert Schwan, Ron Smoire (the Doctor of Cuisine), and August Spier.

Thanks also to Joseph Staretski for pushing me in the right direction; to Rick Clemente for the gastronomic tour of a lifetime; Edmund Assouline for my first chance to be a chef; Phillip and Sharon Simon and Jay and Jackie Korman for being such good friends, and Michael Villella for the tip-off to the Lashers.

My partners have provided enthusiasm and generous support and I thank them. They are Tony Bill, Jeff and Margo Barbakow, Trevor Fetter, and Dudley Moore.

My agents, Maureen and Eric Lasher, conceived of the book with me. I will always be grateful for their confidence.

And special thanks to Sheila Linderman. She has been a partner in this project from the start and has been of enormous assistance each step of the way.

INTRODUCTION

*I*n the late seventies, certain nouvelle cuisine French chefs became celebrities—Bocuse, Guérard, Vergé, the Troisgros brothers—and their cookbooks appeared in English translations. I had just begun cooking professionally, I was an apprentice, really, and I read these books avidly. I found the simplicity of many of the recipes perplexing. When I traveled and ate this "simple" fare at a starred restaurant in France or Italy, or perhaps a handful of such restaurants in the United States, what I got tasted nothing like what I made at home or at work while following these recipes.

It wasn't until my second year as a professional cook that I learned an essential lesson never clearly stated in the cookbooks I was using: Good cooking is not based solely on technique and complexity; it begins with the choice and nature of ingredients. Indeed, the simpler the dish and the fewer the ingredients, the more we must rely on the integrity of the ingredients. Nowhere is this more important than in salad making.

Consider a recipe calling for butter lettuce, olive oil, and vinegar. Unless you know something about lettuces, oils, and vinegars, you might end up with something dismal and bland, as I did when I first began cooking. Today, most of us know that all lettuces, oils, and vinegars are not created equal, but it always bears repeating.

A bottle of mass-produced wine vinegar will not have the same qualities of flavor, depth, acidity, and yes, sweet aftertaste that a vinegar produced by a small maker in France, Italy, or the Napa Valley will. So, the character of a simple salad will depend largely on the character of the olive oil and vinegar, and of course, the quality and handling of the greens.

Salads are not always so simple, but they do have certain qualities in common. Primarily they are made with plants—fruits and vegetables—of one kind or another, and they are served raw or are cooked and usually eaten cold. They are bound and seasoned with a dressing or sauce. As ingredients are added, the salads become more complex. Often we add poultry, meat, cheese, or seafood to the greens. These salads are sometimes called "composed" salads, and they are usually more substantial and filling than a simple green salad.

As our eating habits have changed, reflecting our concern for eating lighter and healthier fare, chefs have sought ways to incorporate all kinds of ingredients into salads. Much of this experimentation has its roots in Southern California, where the salad-as-a-meal has always been well received by those in show business who are exceptionally concerned with their appearance. For example, the Cobb salad goes back to 1936, when it was created by Robert Cobb of the Brown Derby, and was a precursor of today's composed salads. By combining generous amounts of greens with small amounts of bacon, blue cheese, turkey, and avocado, it offered a satisfying meal without being too filling.

Today there are more options in salad making than ever before. Years ago the only choices we had were whether to have mixed greens before or after the entrée, or perhaps to choose between a few more elaborate salads such as the Cobb or a chef's salad. As the world gets smaller, we find ideas from Mexico, Japan, China, France, and Italy influencing our salad making every day. For instance, a chicken salad once meant diced cooked chicken bound with mayonnaise. While it may still mean that, there are many other possibilities at hand.

In what follows, you will find recipes for chicken salads showing influences from the cultures of all the countries mentioned above. Some of these salads are best as a first course, others as a main course, and still others are best eaten between two pieces of bread. The choice is yours.

LETTUCES and GREENS

Of the universe of greens available for salad making, four are considered types of lettuce. The first is iceberg, also known as crisphead. It keeps for up to a week in the refrigerator because it is 90 percent water, which accounts for its lack of flavor. However, its longevity in the crisper is an asset if we haven't shopped for days, and when garnished with a strong, heavy dressing such as Thousand Island or Creamy Blue Cheese, it can be quite satisfying. It also shreds well for tostadas or other types of salads requiring a layer of greens.

The second type of lettuce is romaine. It is also called cos, named after the Greek island where it reportedly originated. The Romans discovered it and brought it to France, where it received the name by which we know it today. Neither the Greeks, the Romans, nor the French knew how to best garnish this wonderful leaf. It took a man named Caesar, in a hotel-restaurant bearing his name in Tijuana, Mexico, to do so seventy-odd years ago. He gave us the Caesar salad, and we've been better off ever since. When preparing romaine, it is best to discard the dark outer leaves, as well as the darker tops of the inner leaves. The crispest, most flavorful part of the romaine is the whitish leaves closest to the core.

The third type of lettuce is the butterhead variety, with tiny, sweet inner leaves at its heart and progressively larger, soft leaves on the outside. There are two principal varieties of this "hearting" category, but each variety has two common names. The first is Boston, or butter, lettuce. They are one and the same. The second variety is Bibb, or Kentucky limestone. They, too, are one and the same. Both varieties lend themselves to lighter dressings because of their soft texture and mild flavor.

The fourth type of lettuce is the loose-leaf variety, including red leaf, green leaf, red or green Salad Bowl, Ruby, and Oakleaf. They share the fact that they do not form into heads, nor do they "heart" like Bibb or butter lettuce. Their leaves are generally curly and large, and they make nice garnishes on platters or around the outer edges of bowls.

In addition to the four types of lettuces, there are many other greens that fill our salad bowl. Spinach is a perennial favorite. For raw spinach salads, try to use small, young leaves. For wilted spinach salads, older, firmer leaves are better because they retain their texture.

Another category of leafy plants is generally called chicory. These are sharp, slightly bitter in taste, and strong in texture. The most popular varieties are Belgian endive, radicchio (red chicory from the Veneto region of Italy), and curly endive, often called chicory in the United States, but referred to as *frisée* by the French. The best frisée is sheltered from light as it grows—a process known as "blanching"—and its leaves are smaller, more delicate, and less bitter than ordinary curly-leafed endive or broad-leafed endive (escarole). These greens, in general, add nice texture and variety to a salad. They work well in warm salads because their texture inhibits wilting. Their slight bitterness complements sweet and sour flavors very nicely.

Arugula, dandelion greens, and watercress are all spicy plants that can give a pleasant, bitter edge to a salad. Arugula, also known as rocket or rugula, is the perfect vehicle for a rich, extra-virgin olive oil and sweet balsamic vinegar. Dandelion is the green of choice for a warm bacon salad. Watercress takes well to mustards and nut oils, and its strong stems can add body to a salad containing other softer leaves, such as Bibb or red leaf.

Lamb's lettuce is a green known by many names: corn salad, mâche (a French name), or lamb's tongue. Its leaves are very soft and mild in taste. Because it is highly perishable, it is expensive. Avoid mixing lamb's lettuce with stronger greens; it will get lost in the tossing, so to speak. I prefer to season it with a drop of nut oil and mild vinegar, and garnish it with other "luxurious" ingredients, such as scallops, lobster, or foie gras.

Mesclun is not a green, but rather a mix of small salad leaves and herbs that once grew wild in various regions of Europe. It is sold already mixed by small specialty growers who take the time to tend the assorted plants. Both rare and costly, it is available in limited supply in some produce markets in large metropolitan areas. It can be simulated by buying a large variety of salad greens, both bitter and sweet, as young as possible, tearing them into small pieces, and combining them with some herbs and edible flowers.

EDIBLE FLOWERS

Edible flowers can add color and texture to many salads. The most popular ones are calendula flowers, which have a slightly bitter quality; nasturtium leaves and flowers, which have a pepperlike quality; rose petals, which have a sweet flavor that blends well with fruits; and violets, which are delicate in flavor and are suitable for fruits and milder greens.

CHOOSING, STORING, and WASHING GREENS

Choose greens that appear fresh and just picked. Avoid those that are spotted with rustlike marks that betray too much time spent out of the soil. They should be stored in the most humid and warmest section of the refrigerator in plastic bags that have holes in them to allow for air circulation. It is best to clean greens as close as possible to the time you are going to use them. However, once washed and dried, though not dressed, they will keep for another twenty-four hours if stored properly.

To wash the greens, fill a sink or large pot with cold water. Trim the greens and tear them into pieces the size you want. There are a few greens that are best cut with a knife: romaine, Belgian endive, and radicchio come to mind. Most, however, benefit from being torn by hand. Put the torn greens into the water and stir them with your hands to loosen the grit and earth clinging to them. This dirt will sink to the bottom and the greens will float. Scoop the greens out before draining the water. (Some greens, such as spinach, may require that the process be repeated with fresh clean water.) Place them, a little at a time, in a salad spinner and spin them dry. This is absolutely the best way to dry greens, and it is imperative that they be dry. Dressing will not adhere to wet leaves, and unwanted moisture will dilute the flavor of the dressing. If you don't have a salad spinner, buy one! They are inexpensive. Failing that, toss the greens in a clean dish towel to absorb the moisture clinging to them. Place them in a bowl and cover with plastic wrap or in a plastic bag. Poke holes in the plastic and keep chilled until ready to use.

OILS and VINEGARS

In salad making, the choice of oils and vinegars is crucial. Regrettably, that choice is confounded by an enormous selection of product with vast differences in cost and quality. What follows will answer some questions many people have, especially about olive oil.

No oil is more commonly loved, versatile, and healthy than olive oil. In the recipes in this book, it appears more often than all other oils combined.

Olive oil is extracted from olives, either a ripe black variety or a partially ripe green one. All olives begin green, and as they ripen they turn black. When the extracting process is done in the traditional and best manner, it involves crushing the olives for the first time between two enormous stone wheels. No heat, steam, or chemicals are used. The oil extracted is called "cold pressed." Since it is the first pressing, the oil is referred to as "virgin" oil. Within the category of "virgin" oil there are quality designations based upon the percentage of acidity in the oil. These are governed by the International Olive Oil Council. An oil can only be called "extra-virgin" if it has 1 percent or less oleic acid. "Superfine virgin" must contain less than 1.5 percent oleic acid; "fine virgin" less than 3 percent; and "virgin" not more than 4 percent. Bottles of fine olive oil ideally claim to be "cold pressed" and "extra-virgin," although sometimes the labels omit "cold pressed" when that process has been used. Beware of mediocre oils in beautiful bottles. Sometimes the best oils come in the plainest packaging. Read the label carefully. All cupboards should have at least one example of an oil of this caliber. In fact, if affordable, one could have a number of such oils: maybe a French variety and an Italian one. French "extra-virgin" oils are often made with ripe black olives, giving the oil a sweet, buttery taste and a golden hue. Italian "extra-virgin" oils are generally made from a blend of ripe and green olives. These oils are fruitier and greener in color than their French counterparts. Oils from Spain and Greece do not have the the delicacy of texture that French and Italian oils have. Whichever fine oil you choose, take care not to heat it. Olive oils of this quality burn at too low a temperature for them to be used in cooking; their flavor would be lost. For cooking with olive oil, choose an oil designated "pure." This oil is from a third or fourth pressing, which usually employs the use of heat or chemicals to assist in further extraction. The oil is then refined to remove the foreign elements used in the process, and receives the designation pure.

The recipes in this book that require a very-good-quality oil will specify extra-virgin. Otherwise, they call for olive oil or light olive oil. Use oil designated pure for these recipes.

Keep your olive oil in a cool, dark, dry place. Kept this way, it will not turn rancid for many months. If you're not going to use it often, buy in small quantities. Flavored olive oil can be made by adding herbs, garlic, and/or peppers to the oil and letting the flavors permeate it. Wash and dry the herbs well. Use ¼ cup to 2 cups of oil. Slightly crush the herbs to release their flavor. Let the oil sit for 2 weeks. Then, strain it into a clean jar or bottle. Add 1 sprig of herb or 1 clove of garlic to identify the flavoring used.

Other oils used in salad making are walnut, hazelnut, peanut, sesame, and such vegetable oils as corn and safflower.

Walnut oil is frequently used by the French. There are some very fine imported cold-pressed French versions whose flavors are superior to those of domestic varieties. Walnut oil blends well with sherry vinegar and makes a good accompaniment to composed salads made with game and bitter greens. Keep it refrigerated after opening.

The best hazelnut oil is also imported from France. It has qualities similar to those of walnut oil, but is a better choice for composed salads made with fish. In such uses, it marries well with champagne vinegar. It also goes well with fruit vinegars. It, too, should be kept refrigerated.

Peanut oil processed in this country is highly refined and has almost no flavor. It is good for sautéing and neutral-flavored basics, such as mayonnaise. French peanut oil has more flavor and adds interest to a vinaigrette.

Sesame oil is available in two varieties. One is a light oil extracted from raw white seeds that is mild and unassertive. It is not the type used in these recipes. The other darker, more flavorful Oriental type is what I use in this book. Because it is quite strong in flavor, it should be used sparingly and cut with another neutral oil such as peanut oil. It is always complemented by lemon or lime juices, as well as rice-wine vinegar.

Vegetable oils, such as safflower or corn, are highly refined and do not have much flavor. They are good for sautéing, and are healthy because they are high in polyunsaturated fat.

Vinegars are the natural complement to oils in salad making. They are usually made from wines (cider vinegar is an exception) that have fermented naturally or turned sour. The origin of the word *vinegar* is the French word *vinaigre*, which means sour wine. The best vinegars are made in old wooden casks formerly used for wine. They are aged for years in cool, dark cellars and are allowed to mellow before they are bottled. Though expensive, they are worth it for their flavor and delicacy.

Any region of the world that produces wine also produces vinegar. Below is a list of the principal vinegars used in salads.

Balsamic vinegar, known in Italian as *aceto balsamico,* is an earthy, highly aromatic vinegar made from sweet wine in the Modena region of Italy. Though it is quite acidic, it has a wonderfully sweet aftertaste. It blends perfectly with good olive oil and usually is used in lesser quantities than other vinegars. It can also be drizzled over fresh fruit, such as peaches or strawberries, for a low-calorie dessert.

Sherry vinegar is made in Spain. It complements nut oils very well. It has a flavor that is at once full-bodied and mellow. Use it in game salads, sweet-and-sour preparations, and preparations calling for bacon, liver, or other rich foods.

Rice-wine vinegar works well with Oriental preparations using ginger, citrus, cilantro, and sesame oil. The Japanese variety is softer and less assertive than the Chinese variety. In some situations where vinegar may interfere with the appreciation of wine, rice-wine vinegar can be used discreetly.

Cider vinegar is great for cole slaw, but its flavor is too harsh for most dressings. It does work well, however, in sweet-and-sour preparations.

White wine vinegar can be made from any variety of white wine, and the consumer usually doesn't know which. It is lighter and sweeter than red wine vinegar and works best with milder-flavored greens, fish, and poultry. Champagne vinegar is a form of white wine vinegar with a more delicate taste.

Red wine vinegar is the most robust of the vinegars. Extremely flexible, it goes well with olive and nut oils. It can be combined with a drop of balsamic vinegar and extra-virgin olive oil to create a quick delicious dressing.

Basic oil and vinegar dressing. There is no simpler dressing for greens. Usually, the proportions are roughly 3 parts oil to 1 part vinegar (or lemon juice). Let your own taste be the final judge. This dressing is best when composed of extra-virgin olive oil and a high-quality red wine or balsamic vinegar. Other good combinations are walnut oil and sherry vinegar or hazelnut oil and champagne vinegar. Minced herbs, such as tarragon, basil, or chives can be added, as well as shallots and/or garlic, salt, and freshly ground pepper. Many of the recipes that follow use this basic framework. For a simple mixed green salad, use 1 tablespoon oil and 1 teaspoon vinegar for each portion. Always stir well before using.

Classic Dijon Vinaigrette. This is a dressing in which oil and vinegar are emulsified with Dijon mustard. Again, the choices of oils and vinegars abound. The French, who originated this dressing, often use a mild-flavored nut oil, such as peanut, with perhaps a champagne or tarragon vinegar. I prefer to use a pure olive oil along with a red wine vinegar. For ½ cup of dressing, the proportions are 1 tablespoon Dijon mustard, 2 tablespoons vinegar, and 6 tablespoons oil. Combine the vinegar and mustard. Season with a pinch of salt. Whisk in the oil, slowly, so the dressing doesn't separate. Season with freshly ground pepper.

A WORD ABOUT SOME OTHER
INGREDIENTS

Herbs. Fresh herbs are always preferable to dried when making salads and their accompanying dressings. However, the fresh version of an herb called for in a recipe may not always be available. There are two possible solutions: Use a dry herb or use a fresh herb, such as parsley, as an alternative to the dried version of the herb in question. If you are going to use a dried herb, it is a good idea to warm it in one of the liquids being used in the dressing. This releases its flavor. The best liquid for this purpose is vinegar. Remember to cool the liquid, whatever it may be, before proceeding to make the dressing.

There are situations in which using dried herbs is inappropriate: for example, recipes calling for herbs mixed in with the greens, or a dish like buffalo mozzarella, tomato, and basil. Fresh basil plays such an integral role that using dried basil would be to miss the point entirely. Here the second solution would be preferred: Find a suitable alternative. Fresh parsley is always available, as are chives. If only fresh will do and it is not available, simply omit the herb.

Mayonnaise. I can no longer in good conscience recommend making mayonnaise at home. As a professional chef, this is hard for me to accept. However, in the last year or so, there have been too many reports of salmonella in raw egg yolks not to take the threat seriously. Commercial mayonnaise, if properly handled and refrigerated, poses no health risk from bacteria. The flavor and texture of store-bought mayonnaise can be improved easily enough to make the result a mayonnaise worthy of a serious cook. Beginning with ½ cup mayonnaise, add ½ teaspoon Dijon mustard, ½ teaspoon good wine vinegar or lemon juice, and 1 tablespoon good-quality oil, such as olive, walnut, or hazelnut. Let the choice of oil, as well as vinegar or lemon juice, be determined by the final use of the mayonnaise. Season with freshly ground white pepper or a small pinch of cayenne.

Onions. Can we imagine cooking without them? The recipes that follow often state "preferably a sweet variety, such as Maui, Vidalia, or Bermuda." In salads, generally, these milder onions are appreciated for their subtlety. Certainly the Bermuda or red onion, though slightly stronger, is widely available and not nearly as dear as the other two varieties. I heartily recommend using it. However, if all you have available is the typical yellow onion, by all means use it. You will enjoy your salad no less; you'll just keep the memory of having eaten it longer.

Green onions and scallions are one and the same. The flavor of the white part is distinctly different from that of the green. Where necessary, the recipes specify which part to use.

Cucumbers. Each cook has his or her preference. Some like the small variety known as kirby, some the waxy American variety; I insist on the European (hothouse) variety. Unlike the other two, its skin is soft, easily digested, and adds color to a salad. Also, its seeds need not be removed.

Lemon and Lime Juices. Lemon and lime juices should *always* be freshly squeezed. Choose fruits with the thinnest skin; they are usually juicier although they may appear smaller. Some types of citrus juicer allow you to extract more juice than just squeezing by hand. Remember to strain the juice before using it.

Tomatoes. Who doesn't have a fond memory of the times when a tomato tasted like, well . . . a tomato? A well-textured, sweet, vine-ripened tomato bursting with its own juices is not easily found today. The chance of finding them are best in the late summer and early fall. Tomatoes should be kept at room temperature; don't refrigerate them. When you are working with a less than ideal tomato, a pleasant way to use it in a salad is to dice it, then season with a pinch of salt, pepper, and a splash of balsamic vinegar.

When good large tomatoes are unavailable, look for cherry tomatoes or Italian Roma or plum tomatoes. They can provide color and texture, though not much flavor. Diced or sliced red pepper offers an acceptable color substitute.

To peel a tomato, cut an *X* at its base. Plunge it into boiling water for 30 seconds. Remove and plunge immediately in an ice bath. Let the tomato cool for 1 minute, then peel the skin, using a paring knife if necessary. Cut out the stem and proceed with the recipe.

Pepper. Pepper is at its best when freshly ground. Where it seems important, some recipes call for white pepper, others black. Still others simply call for pepper. Use white pepper when you don't want black specks in a sauce or dressing. In all cases, even if it is the "wrong" color, try to use freshly ground pepper. When the spicy black husk of the black peppercorn is removed, the remaining kernel is sold as the milder white peppercorn. So, there really isn't much more than a cosmetic difference between the two.

Mainly Greens and Vegetables

Most of these are first-course salads designed to whet the appetite for further courses. Many will enhance a buffet table or serve nicely as a light meal. Garnish chilled Ratatouille, for example, with olives, slices of goat cheese, tomato, and olive oil, and you have a light lunch.

Arugula and Radicchio with Parmesan

Celery, Arugula, Anchovies, and Parmesan

Gorgonzola, Romaine, and Extra-Virgin Olive Oil

Avocado and Watercress Vinaigrette

Avocado, Tomato, and Red Cabbage

Greens with Roasted Hazelnuts, Blue Cheese, and Onion

Caesar Salad

Broccoli and Cauliflower Salad

Fennel with Parmesan

Roasted Peppers with Garlic and Extra-Virgin Olive Oil

Corn and Roasted Pepper Salad

Hearts of Palm, Tomato, Onion, and Haricots Verts

Hearts of Romaine with Thousand Island Dressing

Whole Artichokes with Creamy Herb Dressing

Belgian Endive and Beet Salad with Toasted Walnuts

Belgian Endive with Dijon Vinaigrette

Belgian Endive, Radicchio, and Watercress with Roquefort, Pears, and Hazelnuts

Mixed Greens with Grilled Vegetables

Mixed Greens with Goat Cheese Croutons

Asparagus with Red Wine and Olive Oil Vinaigrette

Leeks Vinaigrette

Chopped Salad of Radicchio, Arugula, Shrimp, Prosciutto, and Cannelini Beans

Creamy Cole Slaw

Tuscan-Style Bread Salad (Panzanella)

Watercress and Mushroom Salad with Bean Sprouts and Roquefort

Watercress Salad with Beets, Anchovies, and Hard-boiled Eggs

Warm Mushroom Salad

White Mushroom Salad

Warm Red Cabbage Slaw with Bacon and Caraway Seeds

Crudités with Garlic Mayonnaise

Dandelion Salad with Poached Eggs and Bacon

Gazpacho Salad

Eggplant Salad

Greek Salad

American-Style Potato Salad

German-Style Potato Salad

Warm Roasted Potato Salad with Raclette Cheese and Curly Endive

New-Potato Salad

Diced Beets with Champagne Vinegar and Scallions

Beets with Walnuts and Yogurt

Cucumber Salad with Dill and Sour Cream

Cucumber Salad with Sesame, Yogurt, and Mint

String Bean and Tomato Salad with Shallots and Tarragon Cream Dressing

Guacamole

Marinated Vegetable Salad

Ratatouille

Mesclun with Chevre and Tapenade Croutons

Macedoine of Vegetables

Celery Root Salad (Celery Rémoulade)

Gingered Carrot Salad with Raisins

Mozzarella Five Ways

Mozzarella with Broiled Eggplant

Mozzarella with Broiled Plum Tomatoes

Mozzarella and Roasted Peppers

Mozzarella with Grilled Radicchio

Mozzarella, Tomatoes, and Basil (Insalata Caprese)

*A*rugula and Radicchio with Parmesan

SERVES 4 AS A FIRST COURSE

I cannot think of a more satisfying or simpler first course.

4 cups loosely packed arugula leaves
1 head radicchio (4 to 6 ounces)
1 tablespoon balsamic vinegar
1 tablespoon freshly squeezed lemon juice
Salt
Freshly ground black pepper
5 tablespoons extra-virgin olive oil
One 2-ounce piece of Parmesan, preferably Reggiano or Grana Padano

1. Remove and discard any large stems from the arugula leaves. Wash and dry the leaves and place in a salad bowl.

2. Cut the radicchio in half lengthwise. Remove the hard white core. Cut each half crosswise into strips the approximate size of the arugula. Add to the salad bowl.

3. Combine the balsamic vinegar and lemon juice in a bowl. Season to taste with salt and pepper. Whisk in the olive oil. Reserve.

4. Using a cheese plane or sharp knife, shave Parmesan into slices as thin as possible, making about 12 or 16 slices. Reserve.

5. When ready to serve, whisk the vinaigrette again and pour it over the greens. Use as much dressing as necessary to coat the greens. Toss well. Lay the cheese shavings on top of the greens and serve at once.

Celery, Arugula, Anchovies, and Parmesan

SERVES 4 AS A FIRST COURSE

2 cups loosely packed arugula leaves, washed and dried
1 stalk, fresh, crisp celery
One 2-ounce can whole anchovy fillets
4 tablespoons extra-virgin olive oil
1 tablespoon freshly squeezed lemon juice
Freshly ground black pepper
One ¼-pound solid piece of Parmesan, preferably Reggiano or
    Grana Padano

1. Lay the arugula leaves in a single layer on a platter.

2. Peel the celery with a vegetable peeler, removing the outer, stringy layer. Slice celery diagonally as thinly as possible, and sprinkle these slices over the arugula.

3. Drain and separate the anchovies. Remove excess oil with your fingers or the back edge of a knife. Lay them randomly over the celery.

4. Drizzle the olive oil and lemon juice over the ingredients on the platter. Season to taste with pepper.

5. Using a cheese plane, shave *thin* slices of Parmesan onto the platter, more or less covering the salad. If you don't have a cheese plane, either use a thin, sharp knife to shave the cheese, or coarsely grate it.

6. Serve at once.

*G*orgonzola, Romaine, and Extra-Virgin Olive Oil

SERVES 4 AS A FIRST COURSE

This is an Italian alternative to the American Hearts of Romaine with Thousand Island Dressing (page 42).

2 ounces Italian Gorgonzola cheese, crumbled (about ½ cup)
½ cup extra-virgin olive oil
1 tablespoon balsamic vinegar
2 tablespoons red wine vinegar
Freshly ground black pepper
1 large head romaine (about 12 ounces)

1. Using a large fork, combine the Gorgonzola with the oil. Do not try to make it homogenous; leave it very lumpy. Stir in the vinegars and plenty of fresh pepper. Let stand at room temperature.

2. Discard the dark outer leaves of the romaine, as well as the dark top third of the entire head. The leaves closest to the core, or heart, are best.

3. Cut or tear the balance of the romaine across the leaves into 2-inch pieces, using the lettuce all the way down to the white part at the base.

4. Wash and spin dry.

5. Combine the lettuce with the dressing. The thick dressing will require more tossing than usual. Serve at once.

$\mathcal{A}$vocado and Watercress Vinaigrette

Let the avocado ripen at room temperature until it is soft to the touch, then refrigerate it until you are ready to use it.

¼ cup minced sweet onion, such as Maui, Vidalia, or Bermuda
1 tablespoon freshly squeezed lemon juice
2 tablespoons red wine vinegar
2 tablespoons chopped fresh basil
½ cup diced seeded tomato
Salt
Freshly ground black pepper
6 tablespoons olive oil
2 ripe avocados
1 cup loosely packed washed and dried watercress leaves

1. Combine the onion, lemon juice, vinegar, basil, and tomato in a bowl. Season to taste with salt and pepper. Stir in the olive oil. Reserve.

2. Cut the avocados in half lengthwise and remove pits. Using a large spoon, scoop out the flesh in 1 piece, or peel off the skin with a knife.

3. Lay each avocado half, cut side down, on a cutting board. Slice crosswise with a sharp knife, keeping slices together as you do so. Using a spatula, place each sliced half on an individual plate.

4. Surround each half with some watercress leaves.

5. Using a slotted spoon, place some tomato mixture over each avocado. Pour the remaining vinaigrette over and around the avocado and watercress. Serve at once.

$\mathscr{A}$vocado, Tomato, and Red Cabbage

SERVES 4 AS A FIRST COURSE

1 cup shredded red cabbage
1 tablespoon red wine vinegar
Salt
1 ripe avocado
1 teaspoon freshly squeezed lemon juice
1 cup diced seeded tomato (about 1 large cut in ½-inch dice)
2 tablespoons extra-virgin olive oil
Freshly ground black pepper

1. Combine the shredded cabbage with the vinegar. Season with a pinch of salt and toss well. Let sit for 30 minutes to 1 hour.

2. Cut the avocado in half lengthwise and remove pit. Cut each half into 6 to 8 strips. Remove skin from each strip, and cut each into ½-inch segments. Carefully place in a mixing bowl (do not crush pieces). Sprinkle pieces with lemon juice.

3. After the cabbage has marinated, drain it and add to the avocado. Add the diced tomato. Drizzle olive oil over ingredients in the bowl. Season with additional salt and several grinds of pepper. Fold together gently and serve.

Greens with Roasted Hazelnuts, Blue Cheese, and Onion

SERVES 4 AS A FIRST COURSE

I am intentionally vague here, calling simply for "greens" and "blue cheese," not specifying which variety of each is best because many types of greens will work, as will many types of blue cheese. I suggest using some greens that are slightly bitter, such as curly endive, Belgian endive, or watercress; a combination is ideal, with perhaps a little Bibb lettuce thrown in for soft texture. As for the cheese, the fine American Iowa Maytag blue would be my first choice, though I would be happy enough with a good Gorgonzola or Roquefort.

⅓ cup (about 1½ ounces) shelled raw hazelnuts
1 small red or yellow onion, preferably a mild variety, such as Vidalia, Bermuda, or Maui
4 teaspoons sherry vinegar
4 tablespoons hazelnut oil
¼ teaspoon salt
Freshly ground black pepper to taste
4 cups mixed greens, trimmed, washed, dried, and chilled
¼ pound blue cheese, crumbled (about 1 cup)

1. Preheat the oven to 375° F. Place the hazelnuts on a baking sheet and bake until the skins are nicely toasted, approximately 6 minutes. Remove from the oven, let cool slightly, and remove as much of the skins as possible by rubbing the nuts within a folded towel. After doing this for a couple of minutes, you will find that most of the skins have come off and you can remove the cleaned hazelnuts from the towel, leaving the toasted skins behind.

2. Crush the nuts into small pieces by pressing them against the work surface with the bottom of a clean sauté pan. Take care not to crush them too much; you do not want crumbs or a powder. Set aside.

3. Peel the onion. Cut it in half lengthwise with the stem facing up. Place the cut side down on a cutting board and cut across the onion, making half circles of each slice. Make the slices as thin as possible. You will need about ½ cup of sliced onion.

4. In a small mixing bowl, whisk together the sherry vinegar and hazelnut oil. Season with the salt and pepper.

5. Place the greens in a large mixing bowl. Add the sliced onion, half the crumbled cheese, and half the crushed nuts. Toss well. Add the vinaigrette and toss again.

6. Divide the salad among 4 chilled plates. Sprinkle the top of each salad with one-quarter of the remaining nuts and blue cheese. For a simpler presentation, toss the salad with the hazelnuts and cheese and serve in a salad bowl. Serve at once.

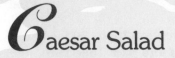aesar Salad

SERVES 8 AS A FIRST COURSE

The best Caesar salad has a combination of perfect ingredients: a good dressing, an excellent-quality cheese, crisp romaine, and delicious croutons. This recipe omits the traditional raw or cooked egg, and is just fine without it.

1 tablespoon red wine vinegar
1 tablespoon minced anchovy (optional)
Salt (optional)
2 tablespoons Dijon mustard
4 teaspoons minced garlic
¾ teaspoon freshly ground black pepper
1 cup olive oil (extra-virgin olive oil, pure olive oil, or a combination)
4 tablespoons freshly squeezed lemon juice
Dash Worcestershire sauce

FOR THE CROUTONS

2 tablespoons light olive oil
2 tablespoons vegetable oil
1 large clove garlic, sliced
2 cups ½-inch bread cubes, made from 2-day-old rolls, 4 large slices French bread, or about ⅓ baguette (the more crust, the better)

3 heads romaine (or enough to yield 4 quarts when torn into 2-inch pieces)
½ cup freshly grated Parmesan (preferably Reggiano or Grana Padano) or Romano cheese or a combination

1. Make the dressing by whisking together the vinegar, anchovy (if desired), mustard, minced garlic, and pepper. Slowly whisk in the olive oil, drop by drop at first. When all the oil has been added, whisk in the lemon juice and Worcestershire sauce. If you omit the anchovy, season with salt.

2. To prepare the croutons, heat the olive and vegetable oil in a frying pan. Sauté the sliced garlic until lightly browned, about 3 minutes. Remove with a slotted spoon. Add the bread to the oil and cook over medium heat, stirring and flipping the pieces often, until golden on all sides. Remove croutons and drain on several layers of paper towels.

3. Remove and discard the outer green leaves of the romaine. The best Caesar is made with the inner light green and white parts of the lettuce. Tear the leaves into 2-inch pieces; rinse and thoroughly dry the lettuce. Count on about 2 cups of torn leaves per person.

4. To assemble the salad, place the torn romaine in a large bowl. Sprinkle with half the cheese. Add the croutons and toss well. Add the balance of the cheese and toss again. Add the dressing, toss well, and serve at once.

Broccoli and Cauliflower Salad

SERVES 4 AS A FIRST COURSE

2 tablespoons freshly squeezed lemon juice
¼ teaspoon minced garlic
6 tablespoons extra-virgin olive oil
Salt
Freshly ground black pepper
3 cups small cauliflower florets (from 1 small head)
3 cups small broccoli florets (from 3 medium stalks)

1. Whisk together the lemon juice, garlic, and olive oil. Season with salt and a few grinds of pepper. Reserve.

2. In 4 quarts boiling water to which 1 tablespoon salt has been added, cook the cauliflower for 4 minutes, until al dente. Remove to a bowl with a slotted spoon.

3. Add the broccoli to the water and cook for 4 minutes, until al dente. Drain and add to the bowl with the cauliflower. Pour the vinaigrette over the vegetables and toss. Let cool and refrigerate for 2 hours, or up to 2 days. Toss again before serving.

NOTE Adding the vinaigrette to the hot broccoli will cause it to discolor, but the broccoli will absorb more of the flavor of the vinaigrette this way. If you prefer, you can cool the broccoli in an ice bath and add it to the cauliflower and vinaigrette just before serving.

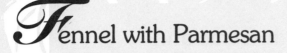

Fennel with Parmesan

SERVES 4 AS A FIRST COURSE

This simple salad is served often in Italy.

2 small fennel bulbs (about 6 ounces each), stalks and leaves removed
4 tablespoons extra-virgin olive oil
2 tablespoons freshly squeezed lemon juice
Salt
Freshly ground black pepper
1 cup (about 3 ounces) loosely packed shavings of Parmesan,
    preferably Reggiano or Grana Padano

1. Using a mandoline or very sharp knife, cut the fennel cross-wise into slices as thin as possible; paper-thin slices are the optimum. Do not use the stem at the base of each bulb. This should yield about 3 cups.

2. Toss the fennel with the olive oil and lemon juice. Season with a pinch of salt and pepper and toss again.

3. Place in a serving bowl. Lay the shavings of cheese over the fennel and serve at once.

Roasted Peppers with Garlic and Extra-Virgin Olive Oil

2 large red bell peppers (6 ounces each)
2 large yellow bell peppers (6 ounces each)
4 garlic cloves
Salt
Freshly ground black pepper
2 tablespoons extra-virgin olive oil
2 teaspoons freshly squeezed lemon juice
1 tablespoon coarsely chopped Italian parsley or fresh basil

1. Cook the peppers directly over an open flame, under a pre-heated broiler or in an extremely hot, dry cast-iron skillet. Rotate the peppers to char them on all sides. Place the charred peppers in a mixing bowl and cover with plastic wrap, sealing the bowl. Or put the peppers in a paper bag, and close the bag. The heat and moisture in the peppers will help to steam off the charred skin. Let the peppers stand for 30 minutes.

2. Peel the garlic and cut each clove in half lengthwise.

3. Cut each pepper vertically from tip to stem. Remove the stem and the seeds. Peel the pieces of pepper under running water, rubbing the skin off with your fingers or the edge of a knife.

4. Slice each pepper half into 5 or 6 strips. Place the strips in a mixing bowl and season lightly with salt and pepper.

5. Add the garlic and other ingredients. Mix well. Chill for several hours. Bring to room temperature before serving.

Corn and Roasted Pepper Salad

MAKES 3 PINTS

¼ cup light olive oil
2 teaspoons minced garlic
2 tablespoons freshly squeezed lemon juice
2 tablespoons dry vermouth or other dry white wine
½ teaspoon fresh thyme, or ¼ teaspoon dried
⅛ teaspoon dried red pepper flakes (optional)
Salt
Fresh coarsely ground black pepper
4 cups fresh white or yellow corn kernels (cut from approximately 6 ears), or 4 cups thawed frozen corn
½ recipe Roasted Peppers with Garlic and Extra-Virgin Olive Oil (page 38), made with red peppers only, diced
½ cup chopped Bermuda onion
½ cup chopped seeded tomato
2 tablespoons chopped parsley
1 tablespoon julienned basil leaves

1. Heat the olive oil in a heavy saucepan over medium heat. Add the garlic, lemon juice, vermouth or white wine, thyme, and, if desired, dried red pepper flakes. Season with salt and coarsely ground black pepper. Simmer for 5 minutes.

2. Add the corn and simmer for 3 minutes. Remove from heat.

3. In a mixing bowl, combine the corn mixture, diced roasted peppers, onion, tomato, parsley, and basil. Chill for at least 2 hours before serving. Adjust the seasoning with salt and pepper.

Hearts of Palm, Tomato, Onion, and Haricots Verts

SERVES 4 AS A SIDE DISH OR FIRST COURSE

This refreshing mix is served alongside the steak tartare at 72 Market Street in Los Angeles. It works well as an accompaniment to simple grilled fish or chicken dishes, as well as standing on its own as a first course.

½ pound haricots verts (thin French green beans; substitute American green beans if these are not available)

Salt

¼ cup diced onion, preferably a sweet variety such as Maui, Vidalia, or Bermuda

1 cup diced seeded tomato (1 large)

One 14-ounce can hearts of palm

5 tablespoons extra-virgin olive oil

2 tablespoons red wine vinegar

1 tablespoon balsamic vinegar

Freshly ground black pepper

1. Trim the ends of the beans.

2. Bring 2 quarts of water to a boil with 1 teaspoon of salt. Prepare an ice bath. Blanch the beans in the boiling water for 2 minutes, until they are cooked through but still crunchy. Drain and plunge immediately in the ice bath to stop their cooking and preserve their color. Drain and cut the beans into ½-inch pieces. Place them in a mixing bowl.

3. Add the onion and tomato to the beans.

4. Drain the hearts of palm. Cut each in half lengthwise and remove the woody center. Cut across the halves to make ½-inch pieces. Add these to the mixing bowl.

5. In a small mixing bowl, whisk together the oil and two vinegars. Season to taste with salt and pepper. Pour the dressing over the vegetables and toss well. This salad is best when served immediately after preparation, but will keep for 1 day in the refrigerator.

Hearts of Romaine with Thousand Island Dressing

Thousand Island Dressing is thick, so it should be used with a firm, crisp lettuce. My first choice is romaine. A wedge of fresh iceberg would also do. This homemade dressing is much tastier than the sweet, commercial dressing.

1 cucumber, preferably European hothouse variety
12 cherry tomatoes
6 cups loosely packed romaine lettuce leaves (2 small heads; use the whitish leaves, close to the center), washed and dried
¾ cup Thousand Island Dressing (page 249)

1. If using European cucumber, cut it in half lengthwise, then crosswise into ¼-inch slices. They will be half-rounds. Cut enough for 1 cup and save the rest for another use. If using a domestic cucumber, peel it, cut it in half lengthwise, scoop out and discard the seeds, then cut it the same way.

2. Rinse the tomatoes under cold running water. Remove the stems. Using a sharp knife, cut each tomato in half. Reserve.

3. In a salad bowl, combine the romaine leaves with the cucumber. Toss well. Add some dressing. Toss again. Add more dressing if needed. Garnish the bowl with the tomato halves. Serve at once with extra dressing in a small bowl on the side.

VARIATION

Eliminate the cucumber and substitute 1 cup Creamy Blue Cheese Dressing (page 246) for the Thousand Island Dressing.

$\mathscr{W}$hole Artichokes with Creamy Herb Dressing

SERVES 4

2 tablespoons freshly squeezed lemon juice
1 teaspoon salt
Four 8- to 9-ounce artichokes
1 cup Creamy Herb Dressing (page 247)

1. Fill a large pot with 2 quarts cold water. Add the lemon juice and salt.

2. Cut off the stems of the artichokes, then cut off the top quarter. With a pair of scissors, trim ½-inch from the remaining leaves to remove the thorns. As each artichoke is prepared, place it in the cold acidulated water. When all 4 artichokes have been trimmed, bring them to a boil in this water. Place a plate on top of the artichokes to keep them completely submerged. Once boiling, reduce heat and simmer for about 45 minutes, or until the leaves can easily be removed but are not falling off. Remove the artichokes from the water and drain them upside down.

3. When cool, pull out the center choke and fibers, using a spoon if necessary. These should come out easily if the artichokes have been properly cooked. A cavity has now been created.

4. Spoon the dressing into the 4 artichoke cavities and serve.

$\mathcal{B}$elgian Endive and Beet Salad with Toasted Walnuts

SERVES 8 AS A FIRST COURSE

⅓ cup walnut halves, (about 1 ounce) preferably freshly shelled
8 heads Belgian endive (3 to 4 ounces each)
1½ cups Diced Beets with Champagne Vinegar and Scallions
    (page 79)
2 tablespoons sherry vinegar
5 tablespoons walnut oil
Salt
Freshly ground white pepper

1. Preheat oven to 375° F. Place the walnut halves on a baking sheet and bake them until they appear toasted, about 5 minutes. Remove from the oven, let cool, and chop coarsely. Set aside.

2. Remove 32 outer leaves from the Belgian endives. Carefully fill the leaves with the beet salad, dividing the salad evenly. Set aside.

3. Slice the remaining endive leaves in half lengthwise and cut them crosswise into ½-inch pieces. Set aside in a barrel.

4. In a small mixing bowl, whisk together the sherry vinegar and the walnut oil. Season to taste with salt and pepper. Add the dressing to the chopped Belgian endive and toss well.

5. Mound the dressed endive in the middle of 8 chilled salad plates. Carefully place 4 beet-filled endive leaves around the mounded salad on each plate.

6. Sprinkle chopped walnuts over the center of each salad and serve at once.

ℬelgian Endive with Dijon Vinaigrette

SERVES 4 AS A FIRST COURSE

4 Belgian endive (about 3 ounces each)
1 tablespoon finely minced chives
1 tablespoon Dijon mustard
2 tablespoons red wine vinegar
½ cup pure olive oil or peanut oil
Salt
Freshly ground black pepper

1. Cut each endive in half lengthwise. Lay the flat side on the work surface and cut across the endive horizontally, making ½-inch slices. Discard ¾ inch of the base of each endive, and place the rest in a salad bowl.

2. Add the minced chives to the bowl and toss well.

3. Make the vinaigrette by whisking together the mustard and the vinegar. Whisk in the oil slowly. Season with a pinch of salt and a few grinds of fresh pepper.

4. Pour the vinaigrette over the endive and chives and toss well. Serve at once.

*B*elgian Endive, Radicchio, and Watercress with Roquefort, Pears, and Hazelnuts

SERVES 4 AS A FIRST COURSE

⅓ cup shelled raw hazelnuts (about 1¼ ounces)

1 ripe pear, preferably Bartlett or Anjou

1 teaspoon freshly squeezed lemon juice

4 teaspoons sherry vinegar

4 tablespoons hazelnut oil

¼ teaspoon salt

Fresh, coarsely ground black pepper

2 heads Belgian endive (3 to 4 ounces each)

1 small head radicchio (about 6 ounces, or 4 inches in diameter), base removed, leaves coarsely chopped

1 cup watercress, washed and dried, large stems removed, base removed, cut in half lengthwise, and coarsely chopped

¼ pound Roquefort or other blue cheese or goat cheese, finely crumbled (about 1 cup)

1. Preheat oven to 375° F. Place the hazelnuts on a baking sheet and roast in oven until skins appear nicely toasted, approximately 6 minutes. Remove from oven, let cool slightly, and remove as much of the skins as possible by rubbing the nuts in a towel. After

doing this for a couple of minutes, you will find that most of the skins have come off and you can remove the cleaned hazelnuts from the towel, leaving the toasted skins behind.

2. Crush the nuts into small pieces by pressing them against the work surface with the bottom of a clean sauté pan. Take care not to crush them too much; you do not want crumbs or a powder. Set aside.

3. Peel the pear. Slice it in half lengthwise and remove core and stem. Dice pear into ½-inch cubes, and toss with the lemon juice. Reserve.

4. In a small mixing bowl, whisk together the sherry vinegar and hazelnut oil. Season with salt and pepper. Reserve.

5. Just before serving, toss the chopped endive, radicchio, and watercress leaves together in a large mixing bowl. Add the crumbled blue cheese and the diced pears. Pour on the vinaigrette and toss well, using as much dressing as necessary to coat the greens. Sprinkle the salad with crushed hazelnuts, and serve at once.

$\mathcal{M}$ixed Greens with Grilled Vegetables

SERVES 4 AS A FIRST COURSE; 2 AS A MAIN COURSE

2 heads Belgian endive
1 Japanese eggplant
1 small zucchini
1 small yellow crookneck squash
1 medium carrot
1 red or Bermuda onion
½ red bell pepper
4 shiitake mushrooms
1¼ cups Garlic-Herb Marinade for Grilling (page 251)
Salt
Freshly ground black pepper
4 tablespoons extra-virgin olive oil
1 tablespoon red wine vinegar
1 tablespoon balsamic vinegar
4 cups greens, such as red leaf lettuce, arugula, radicchio, and
  Bibb lettuce, washed and dried

1. Heat a barbecue grill until very hot. You cannot use a broiler for this dish.

2. With a clean, dry cloth, wipe the Belgian endive and cut each in half lengthwise. Leave the root end on to keep the leaves together.

3. Wash the eggplant and trim off the stem end. Cut into 4 or 5 slices lengthwise, approximately ¼ inch thick.

4. Wash the zucchini and squash and trim off the ends. Slice diagonally into pieces ¼ inch thick and 3 inches long.

5. Peel and trim and carrot. Slice it like the zucchini and squash.

6. Peel the onion. Cut into ¼-inch rings.

7. Using a vegetable peeler, peel the bell pepper as well as possible. The folds in the pepper may not allow for a perfect job, but this is not important.

8. Remove the stems from the shiitake mushrooms. Save the stems for a sauce or stock.

9. Using a pastry brush, baste all of the prepared vegetables on both sides with the garlic-herb marinade. Season with salt and pepper.

10. Grill the vegetables on both sides for about 3 to 5 minutes per side. The object is to give them some color, but not to overcook them. They can be basted with a bit of additional marinade, but do not use too much because they become more absorbent as they cook.

11. Remove the vegetables to a platter as they finish cooking. Cover with foil poked with holes to allow steam to escape. This will keep the vegetables warm, but will prevent them from getting soggy.

12. Whisk together the extra-virgin olive oil and the two vinegars. Add a pinch of salt and pepper. Toss the greens with this dressing. Place the greens in the center of a serving platter. Lay the slices of grilled vegetables around the greens and serve at once.

Mixed Greens with Goat Cheese Croutons

SERVES 4 AS A FIRST COURSE

The croutons will turn ordinary mixed greens into a savory first course. They can be served without the salad as an hors d'oeuvre as well.

Twelve ¼-inch-thick slices baguette
7 tablespoons extra-virgin olive oil
1 clove garlic, peeled
4 ounces fresh goat cheese, such as Montrachet, at room temperature
1 teaspoon chopped fresh basil or tarragon
Freshly ground black pepper
2 tablespoons wine vinegar or lemon juice
½ teaspoon minced garlic
Salt
4 cups mesclun or mixed greens, washed and dried

1. Preheat oven to 375° F. Lay the slices of bread on a baking sheet. Brush lightly with 2 tablespoons olive oil. Place in the oven and lightly brown on both sides. Do not let them get brittle. Remove from oven and rub with garlic clove. Mince what remains of the garlic and reserve for step 4. Turn oven to broil.

2. In a small mixing bowl, mash the goat cheese with a wooden spoon. Stir in 1 tablespoon olive oil, the herb, and a pinch of black pepper. Using the spoon or a small rubber spatula, spread the cheese mixture onto the croutons ¼ inch thick. Cover the croutons completely, including the crust.

3. Place the croutons under the broiler and lightly brown the cheese until it starts to bubble. Turn off the broiler and keep croutons warm under it.

4. In a small mixing bowl, whisk together the vinegar or lemon juice, minced garlic, and a pinch of salt and pepper. Whisk in the remaining 4 tablespoons olive oil.

5. Toss the greens with the vinaigrette. Place in a salad bowl or on individual plates. Garnish with warm croutons and serve at once.

$\mathcal{A}$sparagus with Red Wine and Olive Oil Vinaigrette

SERVES 4

Asparagus vinaigrette makes an elegant appetizer at dinner or a perfect light lunch. This salad looks very nice with sieved hard-boiled eggs over the top.

1 pound medium asparagus (approximately 36 spears)
Salt
1 tablespoon Dijon mustard
2 tablespoons red wine
2 tablespoons red wine vinegar
¼ teaspoon freshly ground black pepper
½ cup olive oil (do not use a heavy extra-virgin olive oil)

1. Have an ice bath ready. If the asparagus are thick, peel them from the tips down the stalks with a vegetable peeler. If they are fine or medium, it is unnecessary to peel them. Tie asparagus into bunches of 6 to 9, putting as many in a bunch as you would serve to 1 person. Cut off the base or woody part at the bottom, leaving about 6 inches of edible spear.

2. Bring 3 quarts water and 1 tablespoon salt to a boil. Place the asparagus bunches in boiling water. Use enough water so that it does not stop boiling when you add the asparagus. Cook the asparagus until slightly crunchy. Fine asparagus should take about 2 minutes to cook; medium, about 4 minutes; thick, about 7 minutes.

3. When the asparagus are done, plunge them into the ice bath. This will stop the cooking and keep them bright green. When chilled, remove from ice water and drain on a towel. Remove the string and set aside until ready to serve.

4. Whisk together the mustard, red wine, and red wine vinegar. Add ¼ teaspoon salt and the pepper. Slowly add the oil, drop by drop at first, taking care to allow the oil and other liquids to emulsify.

5. To serve, arrange each bunch of asparagus on a plate. Spoon some vinaigrette across each bunch without covering the tips. Serve at once.

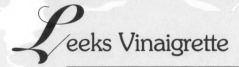

Leeks Vinaigrette

SERVES 4 AS A FIRST COURSE

This dish has been a favorite in French bistros for years, yet it doesn't appear very often on American menus. The dish is easy, healthy, and pure pleasure to those who enjoy simply prepared vegetables.

6 to 12 leeks
Salt
2 tablespoons red wine vinegar
2 teaspoons Dijon mustard
6 tablespoons olive oil or peanut oil
Freshly ground black pepper

1. Bring 4 quarts water to a boil.

2. Cut off the stringy root from the leeks. Also remove all but about 1 inch of the green leaves from the top. Slit each leek lengthwise from the green end to within 2 inches of the base at the white end. Do not cut the leeks completely in half. Rinse each leek under cold running water to remove any dirt gathered in the folds of the vegetable.

3. Tie the leeks with cooking twine into bunches of 2 or 3. This will keep them from falling apart during cooking, as well as make them easier to remove from the water.

4. Prepare an ice bath. Add 1 tablespoon salt to the boiling water.

5. Cook the leeks in the boiling salted water until a knife easily pierces them at the thickest part of the white base. The cooking time will depend on the thickness of the leeks: about 10 minutes for the thin ones; up to 20 for the thicker. Drain and plunge them immediately into the ice bath. Let sit in ice water for about 5 minutes to thoroughly stop the cooking.

6. Remove them from the ice bath and gently squeeze, as you would a sponge, to remove the water they have absorbed. Refrigerate the leeks until ready to serve, up to 48 hours.

7. To make the vinaigrette, whisk together the vinegar and mustard. Slowly whisk in the oil. Season with salt and pepper to taste.

8. When ready to serve, remove the twine from the leeks. Pour the vinaigrette onto the platter or distribute it among individual plates. Place the leeks in the pool of dressing, and serve at once.

NOTE Small leeks are preferable, no larger than about 1 inch in diameter; in that case use 2 to 3 per person. If only large leeks are available, approximately 2 inches in diameter, use 1 to 2 per person.

Chopped Salad of Radicchio, Arugula, Shrimp, Prosciutto, and Cannelini Beans

SERVES 2 AS A MAIN COURSE; 4 AS AN APPETIZER

This is one of my favorite salads. It can be assembled very quickly if you buy cooked shrimp and canned beans. The chopping time for all of the ingredients is short. Also, it makes a great first-course salad at a dinner party because all the ingredients can be chopped in advance and mixed together at the last minute. Cooking the shrimp and beans yourself will produce a tastier salad, but I am not sure it is worth the effort for a quick light dinner for two. On the other hand, if serving it as a first course at a dinner party, you might want to make the extra effort.

4 tablespoons extra-virgin olive oil
2 tablespoons freshly squeezed lemon juice
⅛ teaspoon minced garlic
Salt
Freshly ground black pepper
1½ cups coarsely chopped radicchio (one 5-ounce head)
1½ cups coarsely chopped arugula
¼ pound Cooked Shrimp for Salads (page 256), diced the approximate size of the cannelini beans
2 ounces prosciutto, well-trimmed, thinly sliced, and diced (½ cup)
½ cup Cooked Cannelini Beans (see page 254)
1 tablespoon minced onion (Maui, red, or yellow)
½ cup diced, seeded, *unpeeled* tomato (1 small)

1. Whisk together the oil, lemon juice, and garlic. Season with salt and pepper to taste. Set aside.

2. In a mixing bowl, combine the radicchio, arugula, shrimp, prosciutto, cannelini beans, minced onion, and diced tomato. Mix very well.

3. Add the dressing and mix again. Serve at once.

Creamy Cole Slaw

MAKES 6 CUPS

4 cups shredded green cabbage (see Note)
2 cups shredded red cabbage (see Note)
4 tablespoons grated carrot
1 cup mayonnaise
½ cup sour cream
3 tablespoons sugar
3 tablespoons distilled white or cider vinegar
¼ teaspoon minced garlic
Pinch of salt
½ teaspoon ground white pepper

1. Combine the cabbages and carrot in a large mixing bowl.

2. Whisk together the mayonnaise, sour cream, sugar, vinegar, and garlic. Season with salt and white pepper.

3. Pour the dressing over the cabbage-carrot mixture and toss thoroughly. Refrigerate, covered, for at least 3 hours. Toss well before serving.

NOTE To shred the cabbage, either use a sharp knife to cut very thin (¹⁄₁₆-inch) cross sections, or use a food processor fitted with a 2mm slicer blade.

$\mathcal{T}$uscan-Style Bread Salad (Panzanella)

There are many versions of this salad, all use a combination of ingredients that may include tuna, capers, olives, anchovies, onions, cucumber, peppers, basil, and garlic. The salad invariably contains old bread that has been softened, usually with tomato and very good olive oil.

4 large slices Italian bread, or 8 small slices French baguette that is
    several days old
3 large tomatoes (about 1 pound)
Salt
1 small red bell pepper
2 teaspoons drained capers
½ cup thinly sliced, peeled and seeded cucumber
2 tablespoons red wine vinegar
½ teaspoon minced garlic
6 tablespoons extra-virgin olive oil
Freshly ground black pepper

1. Break the bread into bite-size pieces and place in a serving bowl.

2. Remove the stems from the tomatoes. Chop them into ½-inch cubes. Place the tomatoes and their juices over the bread. Season with several pinches of salt and let sit for 10 minutes. The moisture from the tomatoes will soften the bread. Toss after 10 minutes.

3. Split the red pepper in half lengthwise. Remove the stem, seeds, and core from the center. Cut the pepper into ½-inch squares and add to the salad bowl.

4. Add the capers and cucumber.

5. Whisk together the vinegar and garlic. Season with a pinch of salt. Whisk in the olive oil.

6. Add the dressing to the salad. Season to taste with pepper. Toss well and serve.

Watercress and Mushroom Salad with Bean Sprouts and Roquefort

SERVES 4 AS A FIRST COURSE

Credit should be given to Chef Ken Frank, owner of La Toque restaurant in Los Angeles, for introducing me to this interesting combination of flavors when we worked together years ago.

2 tablespoons sherry vinegar
1 teaspoon Dijon mustard
2 teaspoons coarse-grained mustard
Salt
Freshly ground black pepper
6 tablespoons walnut oil, hazelnut oil, or olive oil
4 medium white cultivated mushrooms
3 cups washed and dried watercress leaves, large stems removed
1 cup bean sprouts
¼ cup crumbled Roquefort (about 1 ounce)

1. Combine the vinegar with the two mustards. Add a pinch of salt and pepper. Whisk in the oil slowly, allowing an emulsion to form. The dressing should be as thick as heavy cream. If it is too thick, 1 or 2 tablespoons water can be added to it. Reserve.

2. Brush the dirt off the mushrooms or rinse under cold water and dry well with a paper towel. Trim bottoms of stems. Slice mushrooms in half lengthwise. Lay the cut surface on a cutting board and cut each half into very thin slices.

4. Combine the sliced mushrooms with the watercress and bean sprouts. Toss well. Add the vinaigrette and toss again.

5. Serve in a salad bowl or on individual plates, sprinkled with the crumbled cheese.

Watercress Salad with Beets, Anchovies, and Hard-boiled Eggs

SERVES 4 AS A FIRST COURSE

16 anchovy fillets
¼ cup milk
2 beets, approximately 2½ inches in diameter
2 hard-boiled eggs
2 tablespoons freshly squeezed lemon juice
¼ teaspoon minced garlic
Salt
Freshly ground black pepper
2 cups watercress leaves, large stems removed

1. Soak the anchovies in the milk while preparing the rest of the salad.

2. Cook the beets following the directions for Diced Beets with Champagne Vinegar and Scallions (page 79) Once the beets are cooked and peeled (through step 3 of that recipe), slice them into ¼-inch rounds and reserve.

3. Coarsely chop the eggs. (Remove the yolks and use only the whites if you are cholesterol-conscious.)

4. Mix the lemon juice with the garlic. Whisk in the oil to make the dressing. Season to taste with salt and pepper.

5. Drain the anchovies, rinse with water, and pat dry; discard the milk.

6. Toss the watercress with the chopped egg, anchovies, and the beet rounds.

7. Add the vinaigrette. Toss again and serve at once.

Warm Mushroom Salad

16 leaves limestone or Bibb lettuce
6 ounces shiitake mushrooms
¼ pound oyster mushrooms
½ pound white cultivated mushrooms
3 tablespoons light olive oil
Salt
Freshly ground white pepper
¼ teaspoon minced garlic
1 tablespoon dry sherry, port, marsala, or Madeira (optional)
1 teaspoon freshly squeezed lemon juice

1. Gently remove the lettuce leaves from the core. Leaving them whole, rinse well and pat dry. Keep chilled until needed.

2. Trim the stems from the shiitake mushrooms, and reserve them for some other use, such as a stock or a sauce (they are too tough to eat). Quarter the caps and reserve.

3. Slice each oyster mushroom into 3 pieces. Do not remove the stems because they are tender. Reserve with the shiitakes.

4. Rinse the cultivated mushrooms under cold water. Remove all dirt and grit, and dry them with a towel. Trim off half of their stems, leaving the other half intact with the cap. Slice these mushrooms ¼ inch thick. Reserve with the other mushrooms.

5. Heat a skillet until very hot. Add 2 tablespoons olive oil and the mushrooms. Season with salt and pepper. Stir well. When the mushrooms soften they will release moisture. Add the garlic at this time. Let the mushrooms continue to cook with the garlic as the moisture evaporates. Add the sherry or other wine, if desired, and cook 1 minute longer. Turn off the heat. Keep mixture warm in the pan.

6. Toss the lettuce with the remaining olive oil and the lemon juice. Lay the dressed leaves on individual plates or on a platter. Spoon the mushroom mixture over the lettuce and serve at once.

White Mushroom Salad

Because this recipe is so simple, you must find the freshest, whitest mushrooms; use only those with caps that are still tightly closed around the stem.

1½ pounds white cultivated mushrooms
Salt
Freshly ground black pepper
½ cup Tarragon Cream Dressing made with olive oil (page 248)

1. If the mushrooms do not have much sand or earth on them you may be able to simply wipe them with a damp cloth. If they need a better cleaning, fill a bowl with cold water and place the mushrooms in it. Stir them around for 10 seconds, letting the dust fall off. Do not let them soak! Scoop the mushrooms out with your hands. The dirt will sink to the bottom of the bowl. Immediately dry them with a clean, dry towel. Gently squeeze all the water out of them.

2. Trim bases of stems, removing the darkened, rough parts at the bottoms. Save these trimmings for a sauce, soup, or stock. Leave about ½ inch of stem. Cut each mushroom in half vertically from the cap through the stem. Lay each half, cut-side down, on the cutting surface. Cut each half lengthwise into ⅛-inch slices.

3. Place the sliced mushrooms in a salad bowl. Season lightly with salt and pepper.

4. Add the dressing, a little at a time, tossing gently. Make sure all the slices are well-coated. Serve at once.

$\mathscr{W}$arm Red Cabbage Slaw with Bacon and Caraway Seeds

MAKES 4 CUPS

This brightly colored warm salad is an excellent accompaniment to roasted meats.

¼ pound slab bacon, rind and excess fat removed, diced (¾ cup)
1 cup chopped yellow onions
4 cups shredded red cabbage (½ medium head), either cut with a sharp knife or with a food processor fitted with a 2mm slicer blade
Salt
Freshly ground black pepper
4 tablespoons red wine vinegar
2 teaspoons whole caraway seeds

1. Heat a large skillet and cook the bacon over high heat until crisp. Remove with a slotted spoon and drain on several layers of paper towels. Reserve.

2. Discard all but 2 tablespoons bacon fat. Reduce the heat to medium and cook the onions in the fat, stirring often, until translucent but not brown. Add the cabbage and season with a pinch of salt and pepper. Cook until the cabbage just begins to soften. Do not overcook.

3. Add the vinegar and cook for 1 minute more. The cabbage will turn bright purple. Remove from the heat and add the caraway seeds and cooked bacon. Toss well. Serve immediately, or serve later, rewarmed over low heat so as not to overcook the cabbage.

*C*rudités with Garlic Mayonnaise

SERVES 8 AS A FIRST COURSE

When putting together vegetables with this savory, garlicky sauce, you are limited only by your imagination and the availability of the produce. What you read here should serve only as an inspiration and guide. Depending on your taste, you may wish to blanch some of the vegetables and leave others raw.

1 bunch radishes with tops (see Note)
1 bunch small carrots with tops (see Note)
8 small white mushrooms
1 small bulb fennel (about 6 ounces)
1 small red or yellow bell pepper
1 teaspoon salt
½ small head cauliflower, or 2 stalks broccoli
1 bunch scallions
1 head Belgian endive
1 small head radicchio
1 cup Garlic Mayonnaise (page 250)

1. Trim and discard the tops and tips from the radishes. Scrape off any dark spots. Reserve in a bowl of ice water.

2. Trim and discard the carrot tops. Peel the carrots. If they are thick, cut them in half lengthwise. Refrigerate until needed.

3. Wipe the mushrooms with a damp cloth to remove any dirt clinging to them. If they are larger than bite size, halve or quarter them. Refrigerate until needed.

4. Remove the fennel stalks and leaves; save them for a soup or sauce. Cut the fennel bulb lengthwise into 8 to 10 slices. Refrigerate until needed.

5. Wash and dry the bell pepper. Cut into ¼-inch rings. Remove the seeds and flesh in the center of the rings. Refrigerate until needed.

6. Prepare an ice bath. Bring 2 quarts water to a boil with the salt. Break the cauliflower or broccoli into bite-size florets. Blanch for 2 to 3 minutes in the boiling water. The vegetables should remain crunchy. Drain and submerge immediately in the ice bath. Leave in the ice bath for 5 minutes to completely stop the cooking. Drain, dry, and refrigerate until needed.

7. Trim the scallions of their beards and the stringy base at root end. Trim the green parts so they are equal in length to the white parts. Rinse under cold water, dry, and refrigerate until needed.

8. Cut the base off the Belgian endive. Separate the leaves. Rinse under cold water, and dry.

9. Separate the leaves of the head of radicchio.

10. Rinse and dry. Line a platter or salad bowl with the radicchio leaves. Lay the endive leaves around the border, then place the assorted prepared vegetables decoratively within the border of endive.

11. Put the garlic mayonnaise in a ceramic serving dish and serve it next to the platter of crudités.

NOTE Try to buy radishes and carrots with tops because if you can observe that the tops are green, you are assured the vegetables are fresh.

*D*andelion Salad with Poached Eggs and Bacon

SERVES 4 AS A FIRST COURSE

½ pound smoked bacon, cut into ½-inch cubes (approximately 1½ cups)
Salt
4 tablespoons white vinegar
4 cups dandelion greens, or 4 cups curly endive (1 large head), green leaves removed
4 tablespoons red wine vinegar
Freshly ground black pepper
4 large eggs
1 tablespoon minced chives

1. Cook the bacon in a hot frying pan until crisp. Remove and drain on several layers of paper towels. Reserve and keep warm on low heat 4 tablespoons of bacon drippings.

2. Bring 1 quart water to a boil. Add 1 teaspoon salt and the white vinegar.

3. Reduce heat to a simmer. Gently break 1 egg into a small shallow bowl. Whisk the water to create a funnel and carefully slide the egg into the middle. Repeat with the other eggs while the water is still moving. The vinegar will help the whites solidify around the yolks. Let the eggs cook at a bare simmer for no more than 4 minutes; it is important that the runny yolks become part of the dressing in the salad.

4. While the eggs are cooking, wash and dry the dandelion greens or curly endive, and mix with the reserved bacon drippings and the red wine vinegar. Season to taste with pepper and toss well. Add the bacon and toss again.

5. Divide the salad among 4 salad plates or 4 low-sided pasta bowls.

6. Remove the eggs from the water with a slotted spoon and place on top of the salads. Sprinkle the chives over the salads; serve at once.

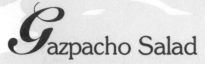

Gazpacho Salad

SERVES 4 AS A FIRST COURSE

A Spanish friend tells me that in Spain, *gazpacho* describes either a cold soup or a salad; each is made with more or less the same ingredients. Here is my version.

3 tablespoons extra-virgin olive oil
2 tablespoons sherry vinegar
½ teaspoon very finely minced garlic
⅛ to ¼ teaspoon very finely minced jalapeño, serrano, or other fresh hot chile pepper (½ pepper or less, seeds removed and discarded)
Salt
Freshly ground black pepper
½ pint cherry tomatoes
½ pint yellow pear tomatoes (these are the size of cherry tomatoes; if they are unavailable, double the quantity of cherry tomatoes)
½ cup diced unpeeled and unseeded European hothouse cucumber (about ½-inch dice) (if the European variety is not available, use the American variety, but peel and seed it first)
¼ cup diced seeded red pepper (about ½-inch dice)
¼ cup diced seeded yellow pepper (about ½-inch dice) (if yellow pepper is unavailable, double the amount of red)
¼ cup finely chopped onion (use a sweet variety, such as Bermuda, Maui, or Vidalia)

1. In a small bowl, combine the oil, vinegar, garlic, and minced chile. Season with a pinch of salt and a few grinds of pepper. Let this dressing sit and develop flavor while preparing the salad.

2. Wash and dry the tomatoes. Remove and discard the stems. Cut each tomato lengthwise into quarters. Place in a large bowl.

3. Add the cucumber, bell peppers, and onion to the bowl. Season with salt and pepper. Toss all the ingredients together while adding the dressing. Serve at once, or chill and serve within 4 hours. Use bowls and spoons for serving.

*E*ggplant Salad

MAKES ABOUT 3 CUPS

Many Middle and Near Eastern cultures have recipes for this dish, as do Eastern and Western European cultures. Serve it as a dip with Middle Eastern flatbread, or on toasted or grilled country bread as a canapé or *bruschetta;* or serve it as a vegetable accompaniment to roast chicken, lamb, or cured meats.

1 large eggplant (approximately 1½ pounds)
1 medium onion
1 teaspoon minced garlic
1 teaspoon salt
2 tablespoons extra-virgin olive oil
2 tablespoons freshly squeezed lemon juice
½ teaspoon freshly ground black pepper

1. Preheat oven to 400° F. Wash the eggplant and dry the skin well. Pierce the eggplant with a fork in four places.

2. Place the eggplant and the *unpeeled* onion on a baking sheet or low-sided baking dish. Bake for about 1 hour, until eggplant pulp is very soft and skin has collapsed completely. Remove from oven and let cool enough to handle.

3. Peel and discard the skin from the onion and chop onion into a paste. Place onion paste in a bowl. Remove and discard the skin from the eggplant, scraping off any pulp that clings to it into the bowl. Chop the rest of the eggplant pulp into a paste, discarding the liquid that accumulates, and add to the bowl.

4. Stir in the garlic, salt, olive oil, and lemon juice. Add the pepper and more salt, if desired.

5. Serve warm or, preferably, chilled. The flavors improve if the salad is allowed to chill completely before serving.

reek Salad

SERVES 2 AS A MAIN COURSE

Since a Greek salad contains only a few essential ingredients, namely feta cheese and olives, those ingredients should be the best that money and time will allow. Let a Greek salad serve as a reason to indulge in the bountiful selection of imported (and domestic) olives available today. Choose three or four varieties from the many you will find in your favorite Mediterranean grocery. Calamata, Atalanti, or the dried brine-cured olives from Greece; cracked green Sicilian or the darker Nanna Ardonio from Italy, or the French niçoise olives are good choices. As for the feta cheese, the four most common varieties available are from Greece, Bulgaria, France, and Israel. The last two are milder, less salty, and less aged. Combining two varieties of this cheese, which is always made from sheep's milk, with a variety of the above-mentioned olives would turn this simple salad into an inexpensive though delightful trip through the Mediterranean.

4 tablespoons extra-virgin olive oil

2 tablespoons freshly squeezed lemon juice

2 tablespoons red wine vinegar

½ teaspoon minced garlic

1 teaspoon chopped fresh oregano (use only fresh oregano; do not substitute dried) or parsley

Freshly ground black pepper

1 small head romaine lettuce

One 4-inch segment from a European hothouse cucumber

6 radishes, trimmed of their leaves and tips, cut in quarters lengthwise

24 assorted olives (as many varieties as possible)

8 anchovy fillets (optional)

1 medium to large tomato, stem removed, cut into 8 wedges

6 scallions, trimmed and cut in half lengthwise

¼ pound feta cheese (one or two varieties), sliced and broken into bite-size pieces

1. Make the dressing by whisking together the olive oil, lemon juice, red wine vinegar, garlic, and oregano. Season with a few grinds of black pepper. Let the dressing sit while assembling the salad.

2. Remove and discard the outer leaves of the romaine. Cut the dark green tops from the center. Break off the base or stem part of the lettuce and tear the remaining light green or whitish leaves into large pieces. Wash and spin-dry enough for 2 generous salads —about 4 cups—and save the rest for another purpose. Place the prepared romaine in a salad bowl.

3. Wash the cucumber segment. Cut it in half lengthwise. Cut each half again, twice lengthwise and once crosswise. This should give you sixteen 2-inch pieces. Add these to the bowl.

4. Add the radishes and olives.

5. Toss the salad with the dressing. Garnish the bowl with the anchovy fillets, if desired, tomato wedges, scallions, and feta cheese.

6. Season with additional pepper, if desired, and serve at once.

$\mathcal{A}$merican-Style Potato Salad

MAKES 3 CUPS

Thanks go to Michael Rosen, my chef de cuisine at Maple Drive, for this tasty version of an American classic.

1½ pounds whole unpeeled baking potatoes (5 medium)
½ cup diced celery (¼-inch dice)
2 tablespoons chopped yellow onion
1 tablespoon chopped sweet pickle
1 hard-boiled egg, coarsely chopped
½ cup mayonnaise
2 teaspoons Dijon mustard
1 tablespoon chopped parsley
Salt
Freshly ground black pepper

1. Boil the potatoes in 2 quarts water to which 1 tablespoon salt has been added. Cook until a knife pierces them easily, 25 to 35 minutes. Remove from water when cooked, and let cool just enough so they can be handled.

2. Meanwhile, combine the celery, onion, pickle, hard-boiled egg, mayonnaise, mustard, and parsley in a medium mixing bowl. Season to taste with salt and pepper.

3. When the potatoes are cool enough to handle, though still warm (so they will absorb the flavors of the dressing), peel them with a paring knife, cut into ¾-inch cubes, and combine gently with the dressing.

4. Refrigerate until well chilled, preferably overnight.

German-Style Potato Salad

MAKES 3 CUPS

1½ pounds unpeeled baking potatoes (5 medium)
Salt
¼ cup chopped onion
⅛ teaspoon freshly ground black pepper
2 teaspoons snipped fresh dill, or 1 teaspoon dried (if fresh is
  unavailable)
2 tablespoons distilled white vinegar
3 strips lean smoked bacon
1 tablespoon sugar

1. Boil the potatoes in 2 quarts water to which 1 tablespoon salt
has been added. Cook for 25 to 35 minutes, or until a knife pierces
them easily. Drain and cool just enough so they can be handled.
Peel them and cut into ½-inch cubes.

2. Place cubed potatoes in a large bowl and add the onion.
Sprinkle with ¼ teaspoon salt, the pepper, dill, and vinegar. Toss
well.

3. Heat a skillet and cook the bacon until crisp. Drain the bacon
on paper towels. Discard all but 4 tablespoons of the bacon fat.
Add the sugar to the pan and cook until dissolved.

4. Pour the hot drippings over the potato mixture and toss well.
Crumble the bacon over the salad and serve immediately.

Warm Roasted Potato Salad with Raclette Cheese and Curly Endive

1 clove garlic, peeled
4 tablespoons olive oil
1 pound baking potatoes (2 large)
Salt
1 tablespoon tarragon vinegar or plain white wine vinegar
1 teaspoon minced shallots
Freshly ground black pepper
3 tablespoons hazelnut oil
4 cups loosely packed frisée (1 large French curly endive)
¾ cup grated raclette cheese (about 3 ounces)

1. Preheat oven to 450° F.

2. Slice the garlic clove into slivers, and add it to the olive oil. Let sit while preparing the potatoes.

3. Peel the potatoes and cut in half lengthwise. Cut each half into 3 strips. Cut each strip in half crosswise. You should have 24 strips, approximately 2 to 3 inches in length.

4. Bring these potatoes to a boil in 2 quarts water to which 1 teaspoon salt has been added. Boil for 5 minutes. Drain and rinse under cold running water. Pat these partially cooked potatoes dry with a paper towel.

5. Combine the vinegar with the shallots and reserve.

6. Place a baking sheet or shallow baking dish in the oven to heat it well.

7. Brush the potatoes with the olive oil and garlic. Season with freshly ground pepper, add to the pan, and roast until they are nicely browned and cooked through, 20 to 30 minutes. Turn them every 5 minutes and baste or brush with the olive oil. The slivers of garlic will also brown.

8. While the potatoes are browning add the hazelnut oil to the vinegar and shallots. Season with salt and pepper.

9. Toss the frisée with this dressing. Evenly distribute the salads among 4 plates.

10. When the potatoes are done on all sides, sprinkle them with the grated cheese. Return to the oven to melt the cheese.

11. Remove from oven and distribute hot potato-cheese pieces around each salad. Serve at once.

*N*ew-Potato Salad

MAKES 1½ PINTS

2 pounds new potatoes
Salt
1 tablespoon Dijon mustard
2 tablespoons red wine vinegar
4 tablespoons extra-virgin olive oil
2 tablespoons minced shallots or yellow onion
1 tablespoon chopped chives or parsley
Freshly ground black pepper

1. Scrub the potatoes well with a vegetable brush. Do not peel. Bring 2 quarts water to a boil with 1 tablespoon salt. Add the potatoes, return to a boil, reduce heat, and simmer 20 to 30 minutes, until a knife easily pierces potatoes. Drain and rinse under cold running water to stop cooking. If you wish to peel them, do so now; I prefer to leave the skins on.

2. Cut potatoes into ½-inch cubes and place them in a large mixing bowl.

3. Whisk together the mustard, vinegar, and olive oil to make a dressing. Whisk the minced shallots or onion and chives or parsley into the dressing. Season with salt and pepper to taste. Pour the dressing over the potatoes and fold gently with a rubber spatula, taking care not to crush the potatoes. Serve chilled or at room temperature.

Diced Beets with Champagne Vinegar and Scallions

MAKES 3 CUPS

This salad tastes best if the mixture is allowed to chill well and the beets have been in the dressing for at least 2 hours.

1 pound beets, tops removed (4 beets, each 2½ inches in diameter)
Salt
2 tablespoons peanut oil
1 tablespoon champagne vinegar
¼ cup finely minced scallions, equal amounts white and green parts
Freshly ground white pepper

1. Wash the beets well in cold water.

2. Bring the beets to a boil in 2 quarts cold water to which 1 tablespoon salt has been added. When the water comes to a boil, reduce heat and simmer until tender, about 30 minutes. The beets are cooked when a knife pierces them easily to the center.

3. Remove from heat and let beets cool enough so you can handle them. Cold water or ice may be added to the pot to speed the cooling.

4. When cool enough to handle, trim both ends of each beet with a paring knife. Peel the coarse skin off and dice into ¼-inch cubes. Place the beets in a bowl and set aside.

5. In a separate bowl, whisk together the peanut oil and the champagne vinegar. Add the minced scallions and season to taste with salt and freshly ground white pepper. Pour this dressing over the beets and toss well.

$\mathcal{B}$eets with Walnuts and Yogurt

MAKES 4 CUPS

This refreshing salad goes well with cold meats, fish, or chicken, and is an excellent foil to spicy Mediterranean dishes.

1 pound beets, tops removed (4 beets, each 2½ inches in diameter)
Salt
½ cup walnut pieces (about 1 ounce)
1 cup chopped Bermuda onion
2 tablespoons walnut oil
1 tablespoon freshly squeezed lemon juice
½ cup plain yogurt (regular, low-fat, or nonfat)
Freshly ground white pepper

   1. Wash the beets well in cold water.

   2. Bring the beets to a boil in 2 quarts cold water to which 1 tablespoon salt has been added. When the water comes to a boil, reduce heat and simmer until the beets are tender, about 30 minutes. The beets are cooked when a knife pierces them easily to the center.

   3. While the beets are cooking, preheat the oven to 375° F. Spread the walnuts on a baking sheet and bake until lightly toasted, about 5 minutes. Remove from the oven and allow to cool.

4. Remove the beets from the heat and let them cool enough so you can handle them. Cold water or ice may be added to the pot at this time to speed the cooling, but do not remove the beets completely from their cooking liquid.

5. Use a paring knife to trim both ends of each beet. Peel off the coarse skin and dice them into ¼-inch cubes. Place in a bowl with the chopped onion and walnuts. Mix well.

6. In a separate bowl, whisk together the walnut oil, lemon juice, and yogurt. Season to taste with salt and white pepper. Pour this dressing over the beets and toss well. Chill for at least 2 hours before serving. The beets will turn the yogurt dressing pink.

Cucumber Salad with Dill and Sour Cream

MAKES 3 CUPS

1 European hothouse cucumber
Salt
½ cup sour cream
2 tablespoons milk
1 tablespoon minced yellow onion
2 tablespoons chopped fresh dill, large stems removed
1 tablespoon freshly squeezed lemon juice
Freshly ground white pepper

1. Cut off both ends of the cucumber. Wash and dry it well. Slice into rounds as thin as possible, using a sharp knife, food processor, or mandoline. Do not peel or seed the cucumber. Spread the slices on a cookie sheet and sprinkle lightly with salt. Let stand for 30 minutes. The salt will cause the cucumber to exude some of its moisture.

2. Meanwhile, whisk together the sour cream, milk, onion, dill, and lemon juice.

3. Pat the cucumber slices dry with a clean cloth or paper towel, removing as much moisture as possible.

4. Combine the sauce and the cucumber. Season with pepper. Stir well. Refrigerate for several hours before serving.

Cucumber Salad with Sesame, Yogurt, and Mint

MAKES ABOUT 3 CUPS

A Middle Eastern–inspired alternative to the pairing of cucumber with dill.

1 European hothouse cucumber
Salt
½ cup plain yogurt (regular, low-fat, or nonfat)
1 tablespoon tahini
1 teaspoon minced garlic
1 tablespoon freshly squeezed lemon juice
2 tablespoons chopped spearmint, or 1 tablespoon chopped peppermint
Freshly ground white pepper
1 tablespoon toasted sesame seeds

1. Cut off tips and wash and dry the cucumber. (If using the hothouse variety, do not peel or seed. If using the regular type, peel, cut in half lengthwise, and scoop out the seeds with a spoon.) Slice cucumber into rounds as thin as possible, using a knife, food processor fitted with a 2mm slicer blade, or mandoline. Spread the slices on a cookie sheet and lightly salt them. Let stand for 30 minutes. The cucumber will exude some of its moisture.

2. Meanwhile, whisk together the yogurt, tahini, garlic, lemon juice, and chopped spearmint or peppermint. Season with a pinch of white pepper.

3. Pat the cucumber slices dry with a towel. Add them to the yogurt sauce and mix. Cover and refrigerate for several hours. Before serving, adjust the seasoning, adding some salt and white pepper if necessary. Stir well. Sprinkle with sesame seeds and serve.

String Bean and Tomato Salad with Shallots and Tarragon Cream Dressing

SERVES 4

Serve this instead of mixed greens as a first-course salad or try it as an accompaniment to cold roast leg of lamb.

½ pound string beans, preferably haricots verts, available in good produce markets (Kentucky-style green beans will work also, provided they are small, young, and tender)

½ teaspoon salt

4 medium tomatoes (about 1¼ pounds)

1 tablespoon finely mined shallots

½ cup Tarragon Cream Dressing, made with walnut oil (page 248)

1. Trim both ends of the green beans and cut them into 2-inch lengths.

2. Prepare an ice bath. Bring 2 quarts of water to a boil with the salt. Cook the green beans until they are tender but still a bit crunchy. Do not allow them to cook until they are yellow or mushy. Remove with a slotted spoon (keep the water boiling) and immediately immerse them in the ice bath to stop their cooking and preserve their bright green color. Drain and dry well with a towel. Place in a mixing bowl.

3. On the end opposite the stem, score each tomato with an X, using a paring knife. Prepare another ice bath. Place each tomato in the boiling water for 15 to 30 seconds. Remove and place in the ice bath. Peel the skin with a paring knife. Cut out the stems. Cut each tomato in half vertically parallel to the stem. Using a teaspoon, scoop out the seeds and liquid from the tomato and discard.

Take the flesh and slice it into ¼-inch-thick strips. Add the julienned tomato to the bowl with the cooked beans.

4. Add the minced shallots. Add a little dressing and toss well. Add more dressing to coat ingredients well. Serve at once.

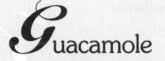uacamole

MAKES 3 CUPS

2 large ripe avocados
1 ripe tomato (approximately 6 ounces)
2 tablespoons minced onion
1 teaspoon minced, seeded fresh, jalapeño or serrano chile
2 tablespoons minced cilantro
1 tablespoon freshly squeezed lime or lemon juice
½ teaspoon salt

1. Cut each avocado in half lengthwise by cutting through to the pit around the entire circumference. Separate the halves. Remove the pit with a spoon and reserve. Scoop out the flesh and place in a mixing bowl.

2. Remove the stem from the tomato. Cut into slices vertically. Cut each slice into ¼-inch strips. Cut each strip into ¼-inch cubes. Add the diced tomato to the bowl with the avocado.

3. Add the remaining ingredients. Mix well. Adjust the seasoning by adding more salt or citrus juice. The spiciness can be adjusted by adding more or less minced chile pepper.

4. Bury the 2 avocado pits in the guacamole. They will help keep its bright green color. Serve with tortilla chips, or serve as a garnish for grilled chicken, fish, or meat.

$\mathscr{M}$arinated Vegetable Salad

MAKES 6 CUPS

This salad, which is first cooked, then chilled before serving, is made in a style the French call *à la grecque.* Omit any vegetable you wish and supplement with more of the other varieties.

4 cups water

1 cup olive oil

1 cup freshly squeezed lemon juice

1 cup white wine

1 bouquet garni (1 celery stalk and/or white of 1 split and well-washed leek that has been folded in half and tied around 1 bay leaf, several sprigs parsley, and several sprigs thyme and/or rosemary)

1 teaspoon coriander seeds, crushed with the back of a frying pan

6 unpeeled garlic cloves, pierced with a fork

1 teaspoon dried oregano

1 teaspoon salt

12 small boiling onions

2 bulbs fennel or celery hearts, fibrous stalks and leaves removed, cut lengthwise into about 8 pieces each (leave base on so pieces will not fall apart)

1 pound uncooked small artichokes, prepared for cooking (page 261)

3 medium carrots, peeled and cut into 1-inch lengths

16 medium white mushrooms, dirt removed and bases trimmed

1. Combine the water, olive oil, lemon juice, wine, bouquet garni, coriander seeds, garlic, oregano, and salt in a large soup pot. Bring to a boil.

2. Add the onions, fennel or celery hearts, artichokes, and carrots. Return to a boil, reduce heat, and simmer, uncovered, for 15 minutes.

3. Add the mushrooms and cook for another 5 minutes.

4. Remove from heat and strain the liquid into a clean sauce-pan. Place the cooked vegetables in a bowl. Remove the bouquet garni and the garlic and discard. Reduce the liquid by half over high heat. Pour the reduced liquid over the vegetables and let cool to room temperature. Cover and refrigerate, preferably overnight, before serving.

Ratatouille

MAKES 1 QUART

Strictly speaking, this is not a salad. Yet served chilled, it is as delightful as any salad and can serve the same function. I use it as a first course, serving it with a slice of good goat cheese and a splash of extra-virgin olive oil, or as part of an antipasto platter, accompanying assorted olives, anchovies, and cured meats. Don't be alarmed by the volume of raw ingredients. By the time the vegetables have cooked down, the volume decreases considerably and the flavors intensify.

2 cups chopped yellow onions
1½ teaspoons minced garlic
½ cup olive oil
2 cups peeled, seeded, and finely chopped plum tomatoes
Salt
Freshly ground white pepper
½ cup cubed red bell pepper
½ cup cubed yellow bell pepper
½ cup cubed green bell pepper
1 cup cubed fennel bulb
1 cup eggplant, skin left on, chopped into ½-inch cubes (one 6-inch Japanese eggplant or ⅓ large eggplant)
1 cup cubed zucchini
1 cup cubed yellow crookneck squash
1 bouquet garni (1 stalk celery cut in half, the 2 pieces tied with string around 12 parsley stems; 1 bay leaf and 6 sprigs fresh thyme or 1 teaspoon dried thyme) added to the onions and garlic in step 1

1. Using a large ovenproof pot that has a lid (an enameled Dutch oven is good), cook the chopped onion and garlic in 2 tablespoons olive oil until the onions are soft but not brown (if using dried thyme, add to the pot with the onions and garlic). Add the tomatoes, ¼ teaspoon salt, and ¼ teaspoon white pepper; cook,

uncovered, for 5 minutes, until the tomatoes are lightly cooked. Set the pot aside with the cooked mixture in it.

2. Preheat the oven to 375° F.

3. In a large heavy sauté pan, sauté the peppers, fennel, eggplant, zucchini, and squash; do each vegetable separately so as not to crowd the pan. Use 1 tablespoon oil with each vegetable. Cook the vegetables very quickly, allowing them to color slightly. Sprinkle each vegetable lightly with salt and white pepper. As each vegetable is cooked, add it to the pot containing the cooked onion, garlic, and tomato mixture.

4. When all the vegetables have been sautéed and added to the large pot, stir well to mix. Add the bouquet garni, pushing it into the mixture.

5. Bring the ingredients in the pot to a boil, cover, and place in the oven for 30 to 40 minutes, or until the vegetables are cooked through but not at all mushy.

6. Remove the pot from the oven. Placing a bowl or another large pot under a colander or strainer, drain the contents of the pot. Remove the bouquet garni and let the mixture sit in the colander with the bowl beneath it collecting the juices for 30 minutes. Place the drained juices in a small saucepan and reduce this liquid over high heat by one-half to two-thirds, until it has the consistency of a thick gravy.

7. Place the vegetable mixture in a storage container and stir in the reduced vegetable liquid. The ratatouille can be served hot at this stage. If storing the ratatouille, let it come to room temperature before refrigerating.

Mesclun with Chevre and Tapenade Croutons

SERVES 4 AS A FIRST COURSE; 2 AS A LIGHT, MAIN COURSE

If you cannot find mesclun, combine such greens as Oakleaf lettuce, mâche (lamb's lettuce), arugula, Bibb, baby frisée, watercress, radicchio, Belgian endive, and baby spinach, to name a few.

Eight ½-inch slices French bread, cut from a baguette
6 tablespoons extra-virgin olive oil
½ cup Tapenade (page 243)
4 ounces fresh goat cheese, such as Montrachet, cut into ½-inch
   rounds
2 tablespoons red wine vinegar
Salt
Freshly ground black pepper
4 cups mesclun, washed and dried

1. Preheat oven to 450° F. Lay the bread slices on a baking sheet and lightly brush them with olive oil (use about 2 tablespoons).

2. Bake bread slices until they turn golden brown. Remove from oven and let cool, but keep oven on.

3. Spread the cooled croutons with the tapenade, using about 1 tablespoon for each. Set aside until ready to serve.

4. Just before serving, place the slices of cheese on a baking sheet and put in the oven to warm and soften, about 2 minutes. Have a spatula handy to remove them.

5. While the cheese is softening, mix the remaining 4 table-spoons olive oil with the vinegar. Season to taste with salt and pepper. Toss the greens with the vinaigrette and divide among the plates. Remove the cheese from the oven and, using the spatula, place the cheese on top of the salads. Garnish each plate with croutons and serve at once.

ℳacedoine of Vegetables

Macedoine is a French cooking term meaning "a mixture of diced fruits or vegetables." This salad is an assortment of cooked vegetables diced into ½-inch cubes and combined with a well-seasoned mayonnaise. Serve this with sandwiches, poached salmon, cured meats, or on a buffet table.

1 teaspoon minced shallot
1 teaspoon wine vinegar
Salt
½ cup diced peeled potatoes, covered with water
½ cup diced peeled carrot
½ cup diced celery or fennel
½ cup diced peeled turnip or celery root
½ cup freshly shucked peas or frozen peas
1 teaspoon Dijon mustard
1 cup mayonnaise
Freshly ground white pepper

1. Combine the vinegar and shallot and let soak together for 20 to 30 minutes while you cook the vegetables.

2. Prepare an ice bath, using a large bowl with plenty of ice.

3. Bring 4 quarts water to a rolling boil. Add 1 tablespoon salt.

4. Choose a strainer that will fit into the boiling water without falling into the pot. Cook each type of vegetable, one by one, in the strainer in the water. When a vegetable is done (tender, but still firm), all the dice can be easily removed by simply lifting the strainer and tossing the vegetables into the ice bath. The approximate cooking times are as follows: potatoes and carrot, 2 minutes; turnip and celery root, 1 minute; peas, 30 seconds.

5. Drain all the cooked vegetables from the ice bath. Pat them dry with paper towels and place in a mixing bowl.

6. In a separate bowl whisk together the shallot and vinegar with the mustard. Whisk in the mayonnaise. Check seasoning and add salt and/or pepper as needed. Fold mixture into vegetables. If possible, refrigerate for 1 hour before serving.

Celery Root Salad
(Celery Rémoulade)

MAKES 4 CUPS

This is an excellent alternative to cole slaw as an accompaniment to sandwiches or on a buffet.

1½ pounds untrimmed celery root (2 bulbs, each 4 inches in diameter)
6 tablespoons freshly squeezed lemon juice
½ teaspoon salt
Freshly ground white pepper
1 cup mayonnaise
1 tablespoon drained minced capers
1 tablespoon brine from capers
1 tablespoon drained minced cornichons
1 tablespoon brine from cornichons
2 tablespoons Dijon mustard
2 tablespoons chopped parsley

1. Trim each celery root with a large sharp chef's knife. Remove all bark and dark spots. You should be left with just white celery root. Cut each into 4 to 6 pieces. Shred celery root with the shredding blade of a food processor or grate it using the largest holes on a grater.

2. Place the celery root in a bowl and toss it with the lemon juice, salt, and several grinds of pepper. Let the celery marinate for 30 minutes to 1 hour.

3. Meanwhile, whisk together the mayonnaise, capers, caper brine, cornichons, cornichon brine, mustard, and parsley in a separate bowl, until well combined.

4. When the celery root has marinated, pour off any liquid that has drained to the bottom of the bowl.

5. Pour the sauce over the celery root and toss to mix thoroughly. Chill well before serving.

Gingered Carrot Salad with Raisins

MAKES 4 CUPS

½ cup raisins
2 tablespoons grated peeled fresh ginger
4 tablespoons rice-wine vinegar or champagne vinegar
1 tablespoon sugar
1 tablespoon freshly squeezed lemon juice
¾ cup sour cream
3 cups packed coarsely grated peeled carrots (about 1 pound)
Salt
Freshly ground white pepper

1. Combine the raisins, ginger, and vinegar and let soak for 1 hour.

2. Add the sugar and lemon juice. Stir well to dissolve the sugar.

3. Stir in the sour cream.

4. Combine mixture with the grated carrots and toss well. Season with a pinch of salt and ground white pepper. If possible, chill 2 hours before serving.

$\mathcal{M}$ozzarella Five Ways

Here are five presentations I've used at 72 Market Street and Maple Drive over the years. I have found that people love mozzarella garnished almost any way, especially when the cheese is the soft, creamy, imported Italian type made with milk from water buffalo. Domestic varieties are often bland and rubbery, though a very fresh domestic mozzarella can be used. In any case, store it in the water in which it comes or in fresh cold water. When possible, remove the mozzarella from the refrigerator about an hour before serving; its flavor improves at room temperature. Smoked mozzarella works well in these recipes also. Again, try to use the freshest cheese available.

By the way, these salads will work equally well substituting goat cheese for the mozzarella. Or, the goat cheese can be marinated for a day or two in a little extra-virgin olive oil with garlic and an herb, such as thyme, oregano, basil, or rosemary. Use the marinade oil instead of the unseasoned extra-virgin called for in the recipes. Mozzarella does not lend itself as well to marinating.

If you are adventurous, try combining several of the following garnishes as one presentation.

Mozzarella with Broiled Eggplant

SERVES 4 AS A FIRST COURSE

1 medium eggplant
Salt
12 ounces Italian buffalo-milk mozzarella or very fresh domestic
  mozzarella
½ recipe Garlic-Herb Marinade for Grilling (page 251)
Freshly ground black pepper

1. Trim off the ends of the eggplant and peel its skin with a
vegetable peeler. From the larger end, cut four ¾-inch-thick slices.
Reserve the rest of the eggplant for another use. Lay the slices on
a sheet pan and sprinkle lightly with salt. Let the eggplant sit for
1 hour.

2. While the eggplant is sitting, slice the mozzarella into
¼-inch-thick pieces. Leave the cheese at room temperature for the
same hour. About 20 minutes before serving, preheat the broiler.

3. When ready to serve, pat the eggplant dry of the moisture it
has exuded. Brush the slices lightly with the garlic-herb marinade.
Season to taste with pepper and broil until browned on both sides
and softened but not mushy, about 5 minutes per side.

4. Remove from the broiler. Place the eggplant on a platter and
surround with the slices of cheese. Spoon some of the garlic-herb
marinade over the cheese and serve.

Mozzarella with Broiled Plum Tomatoes

12 ounces Italian buffalo-milk mozzarella or very fresh domestic
    mozzarella
8 plum tomatoes
4 tablespoons extra-virgin olive oil
Salt
Freshly ground black pepper
1 teaspoon fresh chopped oregano, or ½ teaspoon dried

1. One hour before serving, remove the cheese from the refrigerator. Slice it into ¼-inch-thick pieces and set aside. Preheat broiler.

2. To peel the tomatoes, bring 2 quarts of water to a boil. Score the tomatoes with an X opposite the stem end, using a paring knife. Place them in the boiling water for 30 seconds. Remove and refresh immediately under cold running water. Peel with a paring knife. Remove the stems and slice the tomatoes in half lengthwise.

3. Scoop out and discard the tomato seeds with a teaspoon. Pat the pieces dry with a paper towel.

4. Brush a baking sheet with olive oil. Lay the tomato halves, cut side up, on the sheet so they look like little dishes or cups. Season with salt and pepper and sprinkle with oregano. Broil for 8 to 10 minutes, or until they have softened and started to brown around the edges. When done, remove from the broiler and cover with foil to keep warm.

5. Arrange the tomatoes in the center of a platter. Place the slices of cheese around them. Grind fresh pepper over the cheese. Drizzle the remaining olive oil over the platter and serve while the tomatoes are still warm.

Mozzarella and Roasted Peppers

SERVES 6 AS A FIRST COURSE

1 pound Italian buffalo-milk mozzarella or very fresh domestic
  mozzarella.
1 recipe Roasted Peppers with Garlic and Extra-Virgin Olive Oil
  (page 38)
Freshly ground black pepper to taste
2 tablespoons extra-virgin olive oil (optional)

1. Bring the cheese and marinated peppers to room temperature 1 hour before serving.

2. Slice the cheese into ¼-inch-thick pieces. Lay the slices, overlapping, down the center of a platter. Place the peppers and their olive oil and juices around the cheese. Season the cheese with pepper.

3. If desired, drizzle an additional 2 tablespoons extra-virgin olive oil over the cheese.

Mozzarella with Grilled Radicchio

SERVES 4 AS A FIRST COURSE

Make this salad when you have a charcoal fire going. The flavor of the dish depends on charring the radicchio.

12 ounces Italian buffalo-milk mozzarella or very fresh domestic mozzarella
7 tablespoons extra-virgin olive oil
2 tablespoons balsamic vinegar
Salt
Freshly ground black pepper
2 heads radicchio (4 to 6 ounces each), cut in quarters vertically (do not remove core)
4 leaves very fresh arugula, for garnish

1. One hour before serving, take the cheese out of the refrigerator. Slice it into eight ¼-inch pieces and place 2 slices on each of 4 plates. Heat the grill.

2. Make a dressing by whisking together 4 tablespoons olive oil with 2 tablespoons balsamic vinegar. Season to taste with salt and pepper.

3. Brush the 8 quarters of radicchio liberally with some of the remaining olive oil. Grill the radicchio on all sides until the outer leaves are almost black and the inner leaves have softened and no longer seem raw, about 1 minute per side.

4. Remove the radicchio from the grill and place 2 pieces on each plate, on either side of the sliced mozzarella.

5. Coat each piece of radicchio with 1 to 2 teaspoons of the dressing.

6. Top each slice of mozzarella with a teaspoon of the remaining olive oil.

7. Garnish each plate with an arugula leaf and serve at once.

Mozzarella, Tomatoes, and Basil (Insalata Caprese)

SERVES 4 AS A FIRST COURSE

12 ounces Italian buffalo-milk mozzarella or very fresh domestic
  mozzarella
4 exceptionally fine, ripe tomatoes
Salt
Freshly black ground pepper
8 tablespoons extra-virgin olive oil
8 to 12 large basil leaves

1. One hour before serving, take the cheese out of the refrigerator. Cut it into slices ¼ inch thick. Reserve.

2. Remove the stems from the tomatoes. Cut the tomatoes into ¼-inch-thick slices. Discard the end pieces that are all skin. Season the tomato slices lightly with salt.

3. On 4 plates, alternate slices of cheese with slices of tomato. Grind fresh pepper over them and drizzle with olive oil.

4. Julienne the basil leaves, and garnish the tomatoes and mozzarella with them. Serve at once.

Fish and Seafood

Adding seafood or fish to a salad provides new, more substantial sources of flavor and texture. These dishes make excellent lunch entrees or appetizing first courses at dinner.

Sardine Salad with Capers

Crab Salad with Jicama, Sorrel, and Orange

Crab Salad with Mango, Papaya, and Grapefruit

Crab Louis

Lobster Salad with Corn and Red Pepper

Seafood Salad with Fennel and Red Pepper

Seafood Salad with Saffron and Root Vegetables

Ceviche of Red Snapper and Bay Scallops

Tapenade-Marinated Sea Bass over Fennel and Carrots

Calamari Salad with Artichokes, Olives, and Capers

Smoked Fish with Beets and Cucumbers

Italian Tuna Salad with Olives, Sun-Dried Tomatoes, and Capers

Luncheonette Tuna Salad

Shrimp Salad

Shrimp and Snow Pea Salad with Garlic and Soy Sauce

Barbecued Shrimp Salad

Warm Rock Shrimp Salad with Spinach, Red Bell Pepper, and Bermuda Onion

Cold Poached Salmon with Artichokes, Asparagus, and Roasted-Pepper Mayonnaise

Smoked Salmon with Leeks and Caviar-Cream Sauce

Smoked Salmon, Belgian Endive, and Arugula

Warm Salmon with Citrus Vinaigrette

Seared Salmon Salad with Japanese Vinaigrette

Sautéed Sea Scallops with Arugula, Balsamic Vinegar, and Maui Onions

Warm Scallop Salad

Scallop Salad with Orange, Endive, and Watercress

Herring and Dandelion Salad with Croutons and Bacon

New-Potato Salad with Marinated Salmon and Dill

Charred Rare Hawaiian Tuna Niçoise Salad

Sardine Salad with Capers

Good-quality canned sardines and anchovies are among my household staples. I particularly like those canned by Angelo-Parodi in Portugal. They are widely available in the United States, always packed in olive oil, and not too salty. Such sardines and a jar of capers in the refrigerator can become the core of a simple, quick meal.

½ cup diced unpeeled European hothouse cucumber (½-inch dice)
½ cup diced celery (½-inch dice)
2 tablespoons minced yellow onion
1 medium to large tomato, stemmed and cut into 6 to 8 wedges
2 tablespoons drained capers
1 cup coarsely chopped lettuce, washed and dried
Two 3¾-ounce cans imported sardines, preferably skinless and
    boneless from Portugal
Freshly ground black pepper
1 tablespoon freshly squeezed lemon juice or wine vinegar or
    a combination

1. In a bowl, combine the cucumber, celery, onion, tomato, capers, and lettuce.

2. Drain the sardines of excess oil. Break them up with a fork. Add pieces to the bowl. The olive oil clinging to the sardines will provide the oil for the salad.

3. Season with pepper to taste and lemon juice and/or vinegar. Toss well. The sardines will break up further into bite-size pieces. Serve at once.

Crab Salad with Jicama, Sorrel, and Orange

Here, crab is mixed with a sorrel mayonnaise and served atop a relish made with jicama, sorrel, and orange.

1 tablespoon minced red onion
4 tablespoons mayonnaise
2 tablespoons finely chopped sorrel, plus 12 whole sorrel leaves
1 teaspoon Dijon mustard
1 teaspoon freshly squeezed lemon juice
12 ounces cleaned fresh crabmeat
Salt
Cayenne
1 jicama (approximately 12 ounces)
2 navel oranges
1 tablespoon olive oil

1. Combine the onion, mayonnaise, chopped sorrel, mustard, and lemon juice. Fold mixture into the crabmeat. Season with a pinch of salt and cayenne. Toss gently. Reserve in the refrigerator.

2. Peel the jicama and cut into ⅛-inch-thick strips. Place in a small mixing bowl.

3. Remove the peel and white pith from the oranges. Cut away the segments, taking care not to take any membrane with the segments. Combine oranges with the jicama. Add the olive oil and season with a pinch of cayenne.

4. Cut the whole sorrel leaves into a ¼-inch-wide chiffonade. Reserve.

5. Just before serving, combine the chiffonade of sorrel with the jicama-orange mixture. Place the crab in mounds in the center of 2 plates. Distribute the jicama mixture around the crab and serve at once.

NOTE This salad can be made with diced, cooked shrimp (see Cooked Shrimp for Salads, page 256) instead of crabmeat.

Crab Salad with Mango, Papaya, and Grapefruit

SERVES 4 AS A MAIN COURSE

Here, crabmeat is mixed with cucumber and garnished with a variety of fruits to stretch the costly crustacean.

1 tablespoon rice vinegar
4 tablespoons freshly squeezed lime juice
4 tablespoons extra-virgin olive oil
4 teaspoons grated peeled fresh ginger
2 tablespoons minced scallions, white part only
½ teaspoon freshly ground black pepper
1 tablespoon chopped cilantro leaves, plus 12 whole leaves
1 ripe mango
1 ripe papaya
1 grapefruit, preferably ruby red or pink
1 pound cleaned fresh crabmeat
1 cup julienned unpeeled European hothouse cucumber

1. Make the vinaigrette by whisking together the vinegar, lime juice, olive oil, ginger, 1 tablespoon scallions, pepper, and chopped cilantro. Reserve until needed.

2. Peel the mango and dice it into ½-inch cubes. Place in a small bowl.

3. Peel the papaya, remove the seeds, and dice it as you did the mango. Add to the bowl.

4. Peel the grapefruit, removing its skin and all traces of white pith. Cut away the segments, using a paring knife. Remove all membrane around the segments. Cut the segments in half, and add to the bowl of mango and papaya.

5. In a separate bowl, combine the crabmeat, cucumber, and the remaining scallions. Stir the vinaigrette well and add two-thirds to the crab mixture. Toss gently, taking care to not crush the crab. Keep chilled until ready to serve.

6. Toss the fruit with the balance of the vinaigrette.

7. Mound the crabmeat in the center of a platter or on individual plates. Surround with the diced fruit, lay the cilantro leaves over the fruit, and serve at once.

Crab Louis

Crab Louis is one of those old-fashioned, slightly corny dishes that reminds one of dining in America in the 1950s. For me, it's a fond memory and I gladly provide a recipe for you to try.

½ cup mayonnaise

¼ cup heavy cream, sour cream, or yogurt

1 teaspoon prepared horseradish

4 tablespoons bottled chili sauce

½ teaspoon celery seed

1 teaspoon Worcestershire sauce

4 tablespoons minced scallions

4 tablespoons minced red bell pepper

2 tablespoons freshly squeezed lemon juice

Salt

Freshly ground white pepper and/or cayenne

1½ cups shredded romaine lettuce plus 4 large, whole, unblemished leaves (1 small head), washed and dried

½ cup thinly sliced celery (sliced crosswise)

2 cups cooked Alaskan, Dungeness, or Louisiana lump crabmeat (1 pound), all shell and membrane removed

2 medium tomatoes, stemmed and cut into 8 wedges each

2 hard-boiled eggs, cut into 4 wedges each

1 lemon, cut into 4 wedges

1 tablespoon minced chives

1. Whisk together the mayonnaise, cream or yogurt, horse-radish, chili sauce, celery seed, Worcestershire, scallions, bell pepper, and lemon juice. Season to taste with salt, white pepper, and/or cayenne. Refrigerate until needed.

2. On a serving plate or in a salad bowl, lay the whole romaine leaves, round dark green tops facing out.

3. In a small bowl, toss the shredded lettuce and celery until well-mixed. Lay this mix over the large leaves.

4. Mound the crabmeat over the shredded greens. Garnish the platter with the wedges of tomato, egg, and lemon.

5. Spoon half the sauce over the crabmeat. Sprinkle with the chives. Serve at once with the remaining sauce on the side in a small dish.

$\mathcal{L}$obster Salad with Corn and Red Pepper

SERVES 4 AS A FIRST COURSE; 2 AS A MAIN COURSE

The flavors of lobster, corn, and red pepper complement each other remarkably well, and the late summer months provide a bounty of corn and the most reasonable prices for lobster.

Two 1- to 1½-pound live Maine lobsters, or one 2- to 2½-pound lobster
1 tablespoon butter
½ cup chopped yellow onion or chopped white part of leek
¼ cup chopped peeled turnip
1 cup dry white vermouth or dry white wine
1 small red bell pepper
2 tablespoons walnut oil
1 tablespoon sherry vinegar
1 teaspoon finely minced shallots
Salt
Freshly ground black pepper
1 ear fresh corn, preferably white, or ¾ cup frozen corn, thawed
4 tablespoons heavy cream
2 cups curly endive, as white as possible (1 small head),
    washed and dried
1 tablespoon chopped chives

1. Bring to a boil a pot of water large enough to submerge the lobsters. Once boiling, add lobsters, headfirst, submerging them fully. Simmer (do not boil), covered, for about 8 minutes, or until the shells turn bright red. Remove from the water and let cool on a plate. Discard the liquid. When the lobsters are cool enough to handle, remove the meat as follows: Pull the claws off the body and use a shellfish (or nut) cracker or kitchen mallet to crack them open. Remove their meat, trying to keep it intact. Save all shell scraps. Pull the tail away from the body; crack it open or cut it open using kitchen shears. Pull the tail meat out of its shell. Cut the meat into ¼-inch-thick slices and reserve it with the claw meat.

2. Take all the shells and heads and pound them with a mallet or chop them with a small cleaver to break them into more manageable pieces. Reserve.

3. In a saucepan large enough to hold the shells, melt the butter over low heat. Add the onion or leek and turnip and cook slowly to soften (do not brown). Add the chopped lobster shells.

4. Add the vermouth or white wine and enough water to barely cover the shells. Raise heat, bring to a boil, then reduce heat and simmer for 45 minutes. While shells cook, proceed with other steps.

5. Cut the red pepper in half lengthwise. Remove the stem and as much of the inner ribs as possible. Julienne the halves into $\frac{1}{8}$-inch by 2-inch strips and reserve.

6. In a small bowl, whisk together the walnut oil, sherry vinegar, and shallot. Season to taste with salt and pepper.

7. When the shells have cooked for 45 minutes, strain the liquid into another pan. Press down on the shells to remove all liquid and flavor from them. Reduce this liquid over high heat to about $\frac{3}{4}$ cup. The dish can be prepared to this point up to 24 hours in advance. Refrigerate all components if preparing in advance. Bring them to room temperature before proceeding.

8. Remove the corn kernels from the cob with a knife. Add them to the reduced lobster stock (reheat if it was prepared in advance). Add the cream and reduce again by about half. Remove from heat and cover to keep warm.

9. Toss the endive with the red pepper and the walnut vinaigrette. Place on individual plates. Evenly distribute the pieces of lobster meat among the plates, placing 1 claw on each (2 for a main course). Spoon some of the sauce over each piece of lobster. Sprinkle with chives and serve at once.

Seafood Salad with Fennel and Red Pepper

SERVES 4 AS A MAIN COURSE; 6 TO 8 AS A FIRST COURSE

1 pound mussels

1 pound clams

2⅛ teaspoons minced garlic

6 tablespoons extra-virgin olive oil

2 teaspoons minced shallots or onion

2 cups dry white wine

⅛ teaspoon dried red pepper flakes

½ pound medium shrimp, cooked, shelled, and deveined (see Cooked Shrimp for Salads, page 256)

½ pound lump or backfin crabmeat

1 tablespoon chopped fresh basil

1 tablespoon chopped fresh tarragon

2 to 3 tablespoons freshly squeezed lemon juice

Salt

Freshly ground black pepper

6 cups mixed salad greens, washed and dried (may include red leaf lettuce, arugula, radicchio, Belgian endive, watercress, and/or Bibb lettuce)

½ cup 2-inch julienned red or yellow bell pepper

½ cup 2-inch julienned fennel bulb (use a tender small bulb)

½ cup 2-inch julienned onion (preferably a sweet variety, such as Maui, Vidalia, or Bermuda)

1. Begin by cooking the mussels and clams with 2 teaspoons of garlic following steps 1 through 3 on pages 116–17.

2. Strain the mussel-clam liquid that has collected under the colander. Return it to a small saucepan. Add the red pepper flakes and reduce over high heat by two-thirds. Strain and cool to room temperature. Reserve until needed.

3. Slice the cooked shrimp in half horizontally so that each half still looks like a shrimp. Add to the bowl containing the shelled mussels and clams.

4. Pick over the crabmeat and remove any shell fragments remaining. Add the crabmeat to the bowl with the other shellfish. Return bowl to the refrigerator.

5. In a mixing bowl, whisk together the remaining 5 tablespoons olive oil, ⅛ teaspoon garlic, 3 tablespoons reduced cooking liquid, the chopped basil and tarragon, and 2 tablespoons lemon juice. Check the seasoning, adding salt, pepper, and/or more lemon juice, if needed.

6. Toss the salad greens with half the dressing. Place on individual plates or on a large platter.

7. Add the julienned bell pepper, fennel, and onion to the seafood. Add the remaining dressing and toss well. Distribute the seafood mixture over the dressed greens and serve at once.

$\mathcal{S}$eafood Salad with Saffron and Root Vegetables

SERVES 4 AS A MAIN COURSE; 6 TO 8 AS A FIRST COURSE

1 pound mussels
1 pound clams
4 tablespoons extra-virgin olive oil
1 tablespoon minced shallots or onion
1 tablespoon minced garlic
2 cups dry white wine
4 threads saffron
½ pound medium shrimp, cooked, shelled, and deveined (see Cooked Shrimp for Salads, page 256)
½ pound bay scallops
Salt
Freshly ground white pepper
¼ cup mayonnaise
¼ cup heavy cream
2 tablespoons chopped fresh basil
1 to 2 tablespoons freshly squeezed lime juice
Cayenne to taste
½ cup 2-inch julienned leek, white part only
½ cup 2-inch julienned peeled turnip
½ cup 2-inch julienned celery root (remove bark first)
½ cup julienned peeled carrot
8 large leaves red leaf lettuce, washed and dried, but left whole
4 basil leaves for garnish

1. Scrub the mussels and clams well under cold running water. Remove the beards on the mussels by pulling up and down on them until they release. Discard any shellfish that remain open during the cleaning process.

2. Heat a large saucepan with a lid. Add 1 tablespoon olive oil. Add the clams and mussels, shallot, and garlic. Stir well. Add the wine and cover the pan. Bring to a simmer and let the clams and mussels cook for about 3 minutes with lid on. Remove the lid and any of the open shellfish (place them in a colander over a bowl). Replace the lid and let cook another 2 minutes, until the remaining shells open. Any shells that have not opened by this time are not going to and should be discarded.

3. Drain the cooked mussels and clams in a colander set over a bowl to collect their juices. When they are cool enough to handle, remove them from their shells and place them in another bowl. Chill until needed.

4. Strain the liquid that has collected under the colander and place it in a small saucepan. Add the saffron and reduce over high heat by two-thirds. Strain and cool to room temperature. Chill until needed.

5. Cut the cooked shrimp in ½-inch pieces. Add to the bowl containing the shelled mussels and clams. Return to the refrigerator.

6. Heat a large sauté or frying pan until very hot. Add 1 tablespoon olive oil. Pat the scallops dry with a paper towel. Season them with salt and white pepper. Add to the sauté pan and brown quickly. Do not overcook; they should remain soft in the center. Remove to a bowl and let cool to room temperature. When cool, add to the chilled shellfish, along with any juices that have accumulated in the bottom of the bowl.

7. In a mixing bowl whisk together the mayonnaise, cream, and remaining 2 tablespoons olive oil. Add the chopped basil and 4 tablespoons of the chilled, reduced mussel-clam broth. Add more

(continued)

broth to taste, as well as lime juice, cayenne, and white pepper. Keep chilled until needed.

8. Prepare an ice bath. Bring 1 quart water to a boil with ½ teaspoon salt. One variety at a time, blanch the julienned vegetables for about 30 seconds and refresh them in the ice bath. Drain well and pat dry. When they all have been blanched, toss them with the chilled shellfish and some of the sauce. Continue adding the sauce, little by little, until the entire salad is coated with it and the salad is completely mixed. This mixture can be kept chilled for up to 24 hours. It is best to chill it for at least 2 hours before serving.

9. Distribute the red leaf lettuce among the plates. Spoon equal quantities of seafood salad onto the center of each plate. Garnish with the whole basil leaves. Serve at once.

Ceviche of Red Snapper and Bay Scallops

SERVES 4 AS A FIRST COURSE

4 tablespoons freshly squeezed lime juice
½ pound impeccably fresh red snapper, all skin and bones removed
½ pound impeccably fresh bay scallops
½ teaspoon salt
1 cup diced, seeded unpeeled tomato (1 large)
¼ cup minced onion
½ to 1 teaspoon minced seeded jalapeño (to taste)
1 tablespoon chopped fresh oregano (do not use dried)
1 tablespoon chopped fresh cilantro

1. Place the lime juice in a bowl. Cut the snapper in pieces roughly the size of the scallops. Add the cut snapper and the scallops to the bowl, along with the salt. Toss well. Refrigerate for 1 hour.

2. Meanwhile, in a separate bowl, combine the diced tomato, onion, jalapeño, oregano, and cilantro.

3. When the fish has marinated for 1 hour, mix it well with the tomato mixture. Refrigerate for an additional hour. Serve well chilled.

*T*apenade-Marinated Sea Bass over Fennel and Carrots

SERVES 2 AS A MAIN COURSE

In this salad a mix of fennel and carrot serves as the base for chilled tapenade-coated sea bass strips. If sea bass is not available, Florida or New Zealand snapper would be an excellent substitution.

2 medium carrots
1 fennel bulb (approximately 6 ounces), stalks removed
2 tablespoons dry white vermouth or white wine
2 tablespoons freshly squeezed lemon juice
4 tablespoons extra-virgin olive oil
½ teaspoon minced garlic
Freshly ground black pepper
2 sea bass fillets (6 ounces each), bones and skin removed, cut about 1 inch thick and sliced against the grain into 3 strips each
½ cup Tapenade (page 243)
1 lemon, cut into 6 wedges
1 tablespoon coarsely chopped fresh basil or parsley

1. Peel and trim the carrots. Cut them into 2-inch pieces and then into julienne strips.

2. Cut the fennel in half vertically from the top through the base. Place the cut surface on a cutting board and cut ⅛-inch slices crosswise. Combine with the carrot and reserve.

3. In a bowl, combine the vermouth or white wine, lemon juice, olive oil, garlic, and several grinds of black pepper. Reserve.

4. Preheat oven to 350° F. Place the sea bass strips in a shallow ovenproof pan or baking dish and pour the liquid mixture over the strips. Do not salt the fish. Bake, uncovered, until cooked through

but not dry, about 10 to 12 minutes. Baste the fish with the liquid once during cooking time.

5. When the fish is done, remove pan from the oven. Remove fish with a spatula and set aside on a plate. Pour the cooking juices through a fine-mesh strainer into a bowl.

6. Combine the tapenade with 3 to 4 tablespoons of the cooking liquid to thin it out enough to pour a thick coating over the fish. Bring to room temperature, then cover the plate and refrigerate for at least 2 hours, or as long as 24 hours.

7. Bring 2 quarts water with 1 teaspoon salt to a boil. Blanch the fennel and carrot pieces for about 1 minute. Drain very well and place the vegetables in a bowl. While warm, toss with 4 table-spoons of sea bass cooking liquid. Let the vegetables cool, during which time they will absorb the liquid. Refrigerate, covered, until needed.

8. When ready to serve, place the vegetables on a platter. Lay the strips of sea bass over the vegetables. Garnish with lemon wedges and chopped basil or parsley, and serve at once.

Calamari Salad with Artichokes, Olives, and Capers

MAKES 4 CUPS

This dish is best as a first course, part of a buffet, or part of an antipasto platter.

4 quarts Court Bouillon (page 257)

2 cups ice cubes

1 pound cleaned squid (calamari), a combination of tubes and tentacles

12 cooked Small Artichokes (page 261)

½ cup pitted and quartered Calamata olives

¼ cup drained and rinsed capers

2 tablespoons chopped parsley, preferably flat-leaf

2 teaspoons minced garlic

¼ to ½ teaspoon dried red pepper flakes

4 tablespoons freshly squeezed lemon juice

½ cup extra-virgin olive oil

¼ teaspoon freshly ground black pepper

1. Bring the court bouillon to a boil. Remove from heat and add 2 cups ice cubes and the calamari. Return to heat and cook 2 minutes, never letting it boil. When the calamari becomes firm but not tough, it is ready. Drain and let cool to room temperature.

2. Slice the tubes crosswise into ¼-inch-wide rings. If the tentacles are large, cut them into smaller pieces. Place all of the cut calamari in a large mixing bowl.

3. Drain the cooked artichokes. Quarter them lengthwise, and add them to the bowl with the calamari.

4. Add the quartered olives and capers.

5. In a small bowl, whisk together the parsley, garlic, dried red pepper flakes, lemon juice, olive oil, and ground pepper. Taste and add more red pepper flakes, if desired. Do *not* add salt since the other ingredients are sufficiently salty.

6. Pour the dressing into the bowl with the calamari and toss well. Chill for several hours before serving. Serve well chilled.

$\mathcal{S}$moked Fish with Beets and Cucumbers

SERVES 6 AS A MAIN COURSE

Make this dish with one or more varieties of smoked fish. Sturgeon and trout would be good choices, however any smoked fish will work nicely.

1½ cups Diced Beets with Champagne Vinegar and Scallions (page 79)
1½ cups Cucumber Salad with Dill and Sour Cream (page 82)
½ pound thinly sliced smoked sturgeon
2 smoked trout (about 1 pound each), head, tail, skin, and bones removed; each fillet cut crosswise into 1-inch pieces
Toast or black bread
2 lemons, cut into wedges

1. Use a rimmed serving platter or a low-sided serving dish. Put the beet salad on one half of the platter, the cucumber salad on the other. Lay the slices of fish directly on the salads, almost covering them.

2. Serve at once with toast or black bread, accompanied with lemon wedges.

Italian Tuna Salad with Olives, Sun-Dried Tomatoes, and Capers

MAKES 2 CUPS

I like to make this salad with Italian-style tuna packed in olive oil. Serve it on a bed of greens or as an open-faced sandwich on a baguette.

Salt
¼ cup green beans, cut into ½-inch pieces
One 6½-ounce can tuna packed in olive oil
1 tablespoon drained and rinsed capers
1 tablespoon minced sun-dried tomatoes packed in olive oil
1 tablespoon minced black or green olives
1 minced scallion (equal amounts of white and green parts)
1 tomato, peeled, seeded, and diced
1 tablespoon chopped parsley or basil
2 tablespoons extra-virgin olive oil
2 tablespoons freshly squeezed lemon juice
Freshly ground black pepper

1. Prepare an ice bath. Bring 2 cups water to a boil. Add a pinch of salt. Blanch the green beans for 1 minute. Drain and plunge into the ice bath. Drain and pat dry. Reserve.

2. Drain the tuna of its oil. Place it in a bowl and flake it with a fork. Add the green beans and all the other ingredients and toss well. Season to taste with salt and pepper. Chill before serving.

Luncheonette Tuna Salad

MAKES 1½ CUPS

This "salad without greens" is a classic. It is served in all parts of this country, at lunch counters in drugstores in the South, coffee shops on the West Coast, and luncheonettes in the Midwest. After years of experimentation, trying to achieve at home the flavor I encountered as a kid having lunch with my mom at a corner candy store in the Bronx, I have discovered that it isn't so much the recipe that is crucial, but rather the length of time the tuna salad sits in the refrigerator before eating it. Twenty-four hours is best! A day allows for the perfect melding of flavors and eliminates the "fishiness" that results from a longer time.

One 7-ounce can solid white albacore tuna packed in water, drained
½ cup diced celery (¼-inch dice)
4 tablespoons mayonnaise, or less to taste
1 teaspoon freshly squeezed lemon juice

1. Flake the tuna with a fork, breaking it up as much as possible.

2. Combine with the other ingredients and mix well. Refrigerate 24 hours for the perfect filling for tuna salad sandwich.

OPTIONS AND VARIATIONS

Add any or all of the following:

1 teaspoon minced onion
1 tablespoon sweet pickle relish
1 teaspoon chopped fresh parsley
1 teaspoon chopped fresh dill, or ½ teaspoon dried

$\mathcal{S}$hrimp Salad

MAKES 4 CUPS

This shrimp salad is delicious on canapés, in a sandwich, or on a bed of greens.

Salt
½ cup diced celery (¼-inch dice)
½ cup diced carrot (¼-inch dice)
1 pound cooked shrimp, peeled and deveined (see Cooked Shrimp for Salads, page 256)
1 cup Thousand Island Dressing (page 249)
1 teaspoon prepared horseradish
1 teaspoon freshly squeezed lemon juice
1 tablespoon chopped fresh tarragon or dill
1 tablespoon chopped chives

1. Prepare an ice bath. Bring 1 quart water with ½ teaspoon salt to a boil. Using a strainer, blanch the celery and carrot for 1 minute. Drain and plunge in the ice bath to stop the cooking and preserve the color. Drain. Pat dry, then place in a mixing bowl.

2. Dice the shrimp into ½-inch cubes and add to the vegetables.

3. In a separate bowl, whisk together the Thousand Island dressing with the horseradish, lemon juice, tarragon or dill, and chives. Fold mixture in the shrimp and toss well. Refrigerate 1 hour before serving.

Shrimp and Snow Pea Salad with Garlic and Soy

SERVES 4 AS A FIRST COURSE

1 pound medium (16 to 20 per pound) cooked shrimp, peeled
  and deveined
½ pound snow peas
Salt
½ teaspoon minced garlic
2 teaspoons grated peeled fresh ginger
1 tablespoon minced scallion (white and green parts)
2 teaspoons soy sauce
2 tablespoons olive oil
2 tablespoons freshly squeezed lemon juice
Freshly ground white pepper

1. Slice the shrimp into ¼-inch-thick pieces. Reserve.

2. Prepare an ice bath. Trim ends of snow peas and remove strings. Bring 1 quart of water to a boil with 1 teaspoon salt. Blanch the snow peas for 30 seconds. Remove and immerse in ice water. Drain and pat dry. Reserve with shrimp.

3. In a bowl, combine the garlic, ginger, scallion, soy sauce, olive oil, and lemon juice. Whisk well. Add the shrimp and snow peas. Season with white pepper and toss well. Refrigerate at least 1 hour before serving.

$\mathscr{B}$arbecued Shrimp Salad

1 teaspoon wasabi powder
4 tablespoons mayonnaise
2 tablespoons freshly squeezed lime juice
2 heads Belgian endive (3 ounces each)
1 cup watercress, large stems removed, washed and dried
6 tablespoons peanut oil
1 tablespoon rice-wine vinegar
Salt
Freshly ground white pepper
8 large raw shrimp, shelled and deveined
¼ cup Chinese Barbecue Sauce (page 240)
1 tablespoon julienned Japanese preserved ginger *(sushooga)*

1. Dissolve the wasabi powder in 1 tablespoon warm water. Stir well with a spoon to create a smooth paste.

2. Whisk the wasabi paste into the mayonnaise and add 1 tablespoon lime juice. Whisk well and reserve in serving dish.

3. With a damp cloth, wipe any dirt from the heads of Belgian endive. Slice them in half lengthwise. Cut off the tough core at the base. Slice the halves crosswise into 1-inch pieces.

4. Toss the chopped endive with the watercress and refrigerate until needed.

5. Whisk together 4 tablespoons peanut oil with the remaining 1 tablespoon lime juice and rice-wine vinegar. Season to taste with salt and pepper. Set aside while preparing the shrimp.

6. Heat the remaining 2 tablespoons peanut oil in a sauté pan. Season the shrimp with salt and pepper. Sauté on one side for about 2 minutes. Turn the shrimp and add the barbecue sauce. Simmer for 2 minutes more, making sure to coat the shrimp well. Remove pan from heat and keep shrimp warm in pan.

7. Toss the ginger, endive, and watercress with the dressing. Place on a serving platter.

8. Lay the shrimp on top of the greens and nap them with any sauce remaining in the pan. Serve at once with the bowl of wasabi mayonnaise on the side as a dipping sauce for the shrimp.

Warm Rock Shrimp Salad with Spinach, Red Bell Pepper, and Bermuda Onion

Rock shrimp are small shrimp that are sold already shelled and deveined. They have become widely available, with the invention of a process that allows packers to easily remove their hard rock-like shells before they are shipped to market. Their sweet flavor and firm texture resemble that of a lobster. These features make them a good catch for the cook at home.

1 medium red bell pepper (about 4 ounces)
1 medium red or Bermuda onion
6 to 8 cups spinach leaves
6 tablespoons olive oil
3 tablespoons freshly squeezed lemon juice
¼ teaspoon minced garlic
Salt
Freshly ground black pepper
¾ pound rock shrimp

1. With a vegetable peeler, peel the red pepper as you would a potato. Cut the pepper in half lengthwise. Remove the stem, seeds, and fleshy part inside the pepper. Cut each half lengthwise into 4 strips and cut each strip in half. You will have a total of 16 pieces. Set aside.

2. Peel the onion. Cut it in half lengthwise. Cut the ends off each half. This will allow the leaves of the onion to fall apart. Cut 16 pieces from these leaves, making them about the same size as the pepper pieces. Set aside with the peppers until needed. Reserve the remainder of the onion for another use.

3. Trim the spinach by removing all the stems, including the large stems running through the center of the larger leaves. Wash the spinach at least twice in plenty of water, 3 times if the spinach is particularly dirty. Tear the larger leaves into 2 or 3 pieces. Dry the spinach well and keep chilled until needed.

4. In a small mixing bowl, make a dressing by whisking together 4 tablespoons olive oil with 2 tablespoons lemon juice. Add the minced garlic, and season with salt and pepper to taste. Set aside until needed.

5. Just before serving, heat a nonstick skillet until quite hot. Add 1 tablespoon olive oil. Season the peppers and onions with salt and pepper and cook lightly, just to give them some color (about 45 seconds to 1 minute). Do not overcook them; they should still have some crunch.

6. While the peppers and onions are cooking, toss the spinach with the dressing and distribute it among the serving plates.

7. When the peppers and onions are done, remove them from the pan and place them on the spinach.

8. Return the pan to the stove and heat well. Season the shrimp with salt and pepper. Add the remaining 1 tablespoon olive oil to the pan and cook the shrimp for about 2 minutes. Add the remaining 1 tablespoon lemon juice. Toss quickly and remove from heat. Spoon some of the shrimp onto each plate and serve at once.

Cold Poached Salmon with Artichokes, Asparagus, and Roasted-Pepper Mayonnaise

SERVES 4 AS A MAIN COURSE

I suggest serving this salad as a meal on a warm evening. You can grill or broil the salmon, in which case you will not need the court bouillon; the rest of the recipe is unchanged.

Four 6-ounce portions salmon fillet, skin and bones removed
Salt
Freshly ground white pepper
2 quarts Court Bouillon (page 257)
1 large red bell pepper (approximately 6 ounces)
1 tablespoon freshly squeezed lemon juice
5 tablespoons olive oil
¼ cup mayonnaise
¼ cup sour cream
2 tablespoons minced fresh basil
⅛ teaspoon cayenne
4 medium asparagus spears
1 teaspoon Dijon mustard
2 tablespoons red or white wine vinegar
6 cooked Small Artichokes (page 261)
4 cups mixed lettuce, such as red leaf, limestone, Bibb, watercress, Belgian endive, and/or radicchio, washed and spun dry
2 medium tomatoes, stemmed and cut in 8 wedges each

1. Season the salmon on both sides with salt and white pepper. Place the fillets in a shallow pan suitable for poaching and pour the court bouillon over them, covering the salmon completely. Heat to just under a boil and reduce heat to a simmer. Cook until just done, approximately 8 minutes. Remove pan from heat and let

salmon cool in the liquid. The salmon may be served at room temperature or refrigerated in the court bouillon for up to 2 days.

2. Cook the bell pepper directly over an open flame, under a preheated broiler, or in an extremely hot, dry cast-iron skillet. Rotate it to char it well on all sides. Place the pepper in a mixing bowl and cover with plastic wrap, sealing the bowl, or put pepper in paper bag and close the bag. The heat and moisture in the pepper will help to steam off the charred skin. Let the pepper stand like this for 30 minutes. Cut the pepper lengthwise and remove the stem and seeds. Peel the halves under running water, rubbing the skin off with your fingers or the edge of a knife. Coarsely chop the pepper and place in a food processor or blender. Add the lemon juice and 1 tablespoon olive oil. Purée. Whisk this purée together with the mayonnaise and sour cream. Add the minced basil and cayenne. Season to taste with salt and white pepper. Keep chilled until ready to use.

3. Prepare an ice bath. Cut off and discard the woody bottom quarter of the asparagus. Cut the spears into 1-inch pieces. Bring 2 cups water to a boil with ½ teaspoon salt. Blanch the asparagus for 2 to 3 minutes. Drain and immerse immediately in the ice bath to stop the cooking. Drain and keep chilled until needed.

4. Make a vinaigrette by whisking together the mustard, wine vinegar, and remaining 4 tablespoons olive oil. Season to taste with salt and pepper.

5. Drain the cooked artichokes and quarter them lengthwise. Keep chilled until needed.

6. When ready to serve the salad, combine the salad greens, artichokes, and asparagus in a large mixing bowl. Toss with the vinaigrette. Place this mixture on a platter and lay the drained portions of salmon over it. Garnish the platter with tomato wedges. Top the salmon with the roasted-pepper mayonnaise. Serve at once.

$\mathcal{S}$moked Salmon with Leeks and Caviar-Cream Sauce

This simple salad can border on the extravagant, depending on the type of caviar you use. Sevruga, golden, or salmon caviar all work well, and the recipe requires but one ounce.

3 large leeks (1 to 1½ inches in diameter at base), white part only, julienned

Salt

1 small head curly endive (as white as possible), washed, dried, and torn into bite-size pieces (about 3 cups)

4 tablespoons extra-virgin olive oil

3 tablespoons freshly squeezed lemon juice

Freshly ground white pepper

½ cup sour cream

2 teaspoons finely minced shallots

1 ounce caviar (about 2 tablespoons), or more to taste and budget

6 ounces sliced smoked salmon, gray parts removed (about 4 large slices)

1 tablespoon chopped chives

1. Prepare an ice bath. Bring 1 quart water to a boil with ½ teaspoon salt. Add the leeks and cook for about 3 minutes, until tender. Drain and plunge immediately into the ice bath. When cool, drain and pat dry with paper towels. In a bowl, combine the leeks and endive, separating the strands of leek to mix evenly with the endive pieces.

2. In a small bowl, whisk together the olive oil and 2 tablespoons lemon juice. Season with salt and pepper to taste. Set aside.

3. In another small bowl, whisk together the sour cream, shallots, and the remaining 1 tablespoon lemon juice. Season with white pepper (do not add salt). Fold in the caviar.

4. Toss the curly endive and leeks with the olive oil dressing. Divide among 4 plates. Lay the salmon slices over the greens. Drizzle the caviar-sour cream sauce over the salmon. Sprinkle with chives and serve immediately.

Smoked Salmon, Belgian Endive, and Arugula

SERVES 4 AS AN APPETIZER; 2 AS A MAIN COURSE

6 ounces Scottish or Norwegian smoked salmon, cut into julienne strips (¾ cup)
2 cups diagonally sliced Belgian endive (3 ounces each)
2 cups loosely packed arugula leaves, washed and dried
1 tablespoon finely minced chives
Generous amount freshly ground black pepper
2 tablespoons extra-virgin olive oil
4 teaspoons freshly squeezed lemon juice

1. Place the salmon, endive, and arugula in a serving bowl.

2. Add the chives, pepper, oil, and lemon juice. Toss well. Serve immediately.

_W_arm Salmon Salad with Citrus Vinaigrette

12 ounces salmon fillet, skin and bones removed
5 tablespoons olive oil
Salt
Freshly ground white pepper
1 tablespoon sherry vinegar
1 tablespoon soy sauce
⅛ teaspoon cayenne
2 drops Tabasco
1 tablespoon freshly squeezed lemon juice
1 tablespoon freshly squeezed lime juice
2 tablespoons grapefruit juice
2 tablespoons freshly squeezed orange juice
1 teaspoon chopped peeled fresh ginger
1 head curly endive (frisée), or 4 cups mixed greens, washed and dried
1 tablespoon chopped chervil or Italian parsley
1 tablespoons chopped chives
1 tablespoon chopped cilantro

1. With a very sharp knife, cut the salmon against the grain into ¼-inch slices. Brush both sides of each slice with 1 tablespoon of the olive oil. Season with salt and white pepper. Roll each slice into a "rosette," pinching one end of the roll and opening the other. Refrigerate while preparing the other ingredients. Preheat broiler.

2. Prepare the vinaigrette by whisking together the sherry vinegar, soy sauce, cayenne, Tabasco, citrus juices, and ginger. Slowly whisk in the remaining 4 tablespoons olive oil. Season to taste with white pepper.

3. Toss the greens with 6 to 8 tablespoons of the vinaigrette, and divide among 4 plates or place on a large serving platter.

4. Place the salmon on a broiler pan and broil for about 45 seconds to 1 minute, or until just cooked. With a spatula, place the salmon rosettes on the greens.

5. Nap the rosettes with the remaining vinaigrette and sprinkle with the chopped herbs. Serve at once.

Seared Salmon Salad with Japanese Vinaigrette

SERVES 4 AS A FIRST COURSE

8 ounces fresh salmon fillet
3 heads Belgian endive
1 teaspoon olive oil or vegetable oil
Salt
Freshly ground white pepper
3 cups watercress leaves, washed and dried, large stems removed
½ cup Japanese Vinaigrette (page 245)
1 tablespoon minced chives

1. Cut the salmon against the grain into ¼-inch slices.

2. Cut the endive in half lengthwise. Remove and discard the core at the base. Cut the leaves diagonally into long strips about ½ inch wide. Combine with the watercress and reserve.

3. Heat a nonstick skillet until very hot. Add the oil. Season the slices of salmon with salt and white pepper. Sear for 20 to 30 seconds on each side. Remove slices to a plate.

4. Mix the greens with 6 tablespoons vinaigrette. Arrange on a platter. Lay the slices of salmon over the greens, and top with the remaining vinaigrette. Sprinkle with chives and serve at once.

Sautéed Sea Scallops with Arugula, Balsamic Vinegar, and Maui Onions

SERVES 2 AS AN APPETIZER OR FIRST COURSE

2 cups loosely packed arugula leaves, washed and well dried, large
   stems removed
3 tablespoons extra-virgin olive oil
1 tablespoon freshly squeezed lemon juice
Freshly ground black pepper
½ cup sliced Maui onion or other sweet onion such as Vidalia
   or Bermuda (1 small)
Salt
4 ounces very fresh sea scallops, cut into ¼-inch slices
1 tablespoon balsamic vinegar

1. Toss the arugula with 2 tablespoons olive oil, the lemon juice, and a generous amount of freshly ground pepper. Divide between 2 plates.

2. Heat a well-seasoned or nonstick sauté pan until quite hot. Add the remaining 1 tablespoon olive oil and the onion. Sprinkle with a pinch of salt and several grinds of pepper. Cook the onion slices for about 1 minute, long enough for them to soften slightly, but not enough for them to lose their crunch.

3. Add the scallops to the pan and toss with the onion just long enough to cook the scallops medium-rare, about 30 to 45 seconds.

4. Add the balsamic vinegar and toss.

5. Divide the scallop mixture between the 2 plates, on top of the arugula. Serve at once.

Warm Scallop Salad

Salt
20 snow peas, stems removed
3 tablespoons olive oil
3 tablespoons plus 1 teaspoon peanut oil
1½ tablespoons soy sauce
1½ tablespoons freshly squeezed lemon juice
Freshly ground white pepper
2 cups watercress, washed and dried, heavy stems removed
4 cups red leaf lettuce torn into pieces, rinsed, and dried
1 tablespoon chopped chives
½ pound cleaned bay scallops
4 shiitake mushrooms, stems removed and julienned
1 medium-size tart green apple, peeled, cored, and diced into
    ¼-inch cubes
¼ cup toasted slivered almonds

1. Prepare an ice bath. Bring 2 cups water to a boil with ½ teaspoon salt. Add the snow peas and blanch for 20 seconds. Drain and immediately plunge into ice bath to preserve the color and stop the cooking. Drain and set aside.

2. Make the dressing by whisking together the olive oil, 3 tablespoons peanut oil, soy sauce, and lemon juice. Season to taste with ground white pepper. No salt will be necessary.

3. Mix together the watercress and red leaf lettuce in a bowl, and toss with half of the chives. Add about three-quarters of the dressing (just enough to coat the leaves) and toss again. Divide the greens among 4 plates.

4. Heat a skillet until very, very hot. Add remaining 1 teaspoon peanut oil. Season the scallops and shiitakes with salt and pepper and add them to the skillet. Sauté over high heat until half-cooked, about 30 seconds; remove to a small bowl. Add the apple cubes, almonds, snow peas, and the remaining chives. Toss with the remaining dressing. Divide the scallop mixture among the 4 plates, placing it on top of the greens. Serve immediately.

Scallop Salad with Orange, Endive, and Watercress

When fresh scallops are sautéed over high heat and then allowed to sit for 10 minutes, they exude their juices, which are combined with other ingredients to create a vinaigrette for this salad. The scallops are served at room temperature.

2 tablespoons freshly squeezed orange juice
2 tablespoons sherry vinegar
½ teaspoon minced garlic
1 tablespoon minced shallots
½ pound large sea scallops, muscle removed
Salt
Freshly ground black pepper
4 tablespoons extra-virgin olive oil
½ cup orange segments, preferably navel oranges, all skin and
    pith removed
1 teaspoon minced chives
2 cups loosely packed watercress leaves, washed and dried, large
    stems removed
2 cups julienned Belgian endive (about 2 heads endive, base removed
    and cut lengthwise from tip to bottom)

1. In a small bowl, combine the orange juice, vinegar, garlic, and shallots.

2. Place a strainer over a bowl. Pat the scallops dry and season with salt and pepper to taste. Heat a sauté pan until very hot. Add 2 tablespoons oil, then the scallops and sauté until light brown on all sides, about 1 to 1½ minutes. Do not overcook; their centers should remain soft and undercooked. When just done, add the orange juice mixture. Cook for 15 seconds, then strain over a bowl.

Using a rubber spatula, scrape any remaining juices from the pan into the strainer. Let the scallops sit in the strainer for 10 minutes.

3. Remove the strainer from the bowl and set the scallops aside. Whisk the remaining 2 tablespoons olive oil into the collected juices. Taste. Add a splash of vinegar or orange juice, if needed. Season with salt and pepper to taste.

4. Slice the scallops into rounds ¼ inch thick. Combine with orange segments and chives. Season with 2 tablespoons of vinaigrette.

5. Combine the watercress and endive in a bowl. Toss with the balance of the vinaigrette. Place on individual plates and flatten slightly. Spoon the scallop-orange mixture on the center of each salad and serve at once.

Herring and Dandelion Salad with Croutons and Bacon

SERVES 4 AS A FIRST COURSE

FOR THE CROUTONS

2 tablespoons vegetable oil or olive oil

1 tablespoon butter

1 clove garlic, peeled and sliced

1 cup ½-inch French bread cubes from day-old bread (use 2 large slices, 1 small roll, or a 4-inch piece of baguette)

FOR THE SALAD

¼ pound smoked slab bacon, rind removed, cut into ¼-inch dice (¾ cup)

2 tablespoons sherry vinegar

2 tablespoons Dijon mustard

2 tablespoons walnut oil

Freshly ground black pepper

4 cups dandelion greens, washed and dried

½ pound pickled herring, skin and bones removed, cut into ¼-inch strips

2 hard-boiled eggs, coarsely chopped

1. Heat the vegetable oil or olive oil and butter in a frying pan. Sauté the garlic until very lightly browned, about 3 minutes. Remove the garlic with a slotted spoon and discard. Add the cubed

bread and cook over medium heat, stirring often, until golden brown on all sides. Remove with a slotted spoon and drain on several layers of paper towels. Reserve.

2. Blanch the bacon for 5 minutes in 1 quart of simmering water. Drain and rinse under cold water.

3. Combine the vinegar and mustard, and reserve.

4. Heat the walnut oil in a frying pan and cook the bacon until brown. Remove the bacon with a slotted spoon and drain on paper towels. Reserve the pan drippings.

5. Whisk 4 tablespoons drippings into the vinegar and mustard. Season with plenty of pepper, but no salt.

6. Combine the greens, bacon, and herring in a large bowl. Add the vinaigrette and toss well. Add the croutons and toss again. Sprinkle with chopped egg and serve at once.

New-Potato Salad with Marinated Salmon and Dill

SERVES 4 AS A FIRST COURSE; 2 AS A MAIN COURSE

This salad may be served warm, at the time the potatoes are cooked, or chilled, at a later time. I prefer this warm.

1 tablespoon Dijon mustard
2 tablespoons champagne vinegar
4 tablespoons peanut oil or olive oil
2 tablespoons minced shallots or yellow onion
2 tablespoons marinated salmon juices, see Marinated Salmon (page 260)
2 tablespoons minced fresh dill
Salt
Freshly ground black pepper
1 pound new potatoes, preferably Yellow Finn or other small potato, such as Red Rose
12 thin slices Marinated Salmon (page 260) or smoked salmon
4 dill sprigs for garnish
1 lemon cut into 4 wedges

1. Whisk together the mustard and vinegar. Slowly add the oil, whisking to form an emulsion. Add the shallots, salmon juices (if using smoked salmon, substitute 1 tablespoon lemon juice and 1 tablespoon water), and minced dill. Season with salt and pepper to taste.

2. Scrub the potatoes well with a vegetable brush. Do not peel. Bring 1½ quarts water to a boil with 1 teaspoon salt. Add the potatoes, return to a boil, and reduce heat to simmer for 20 to 30 minutes, until a knife easily pierces them. Drain and cool. When cool enough to handle, slice into ¼-inch rounds (do not peel).

3. In a mixing bowl, combine the potato slices with half the vinaigrette. Toss gently to avoid breaking the potatoes. Place on a platter or on individual plates. Lay the slices of salmon over the potatoes. Garnish with the dill sprigs and lemon wedges. Serve at once with the extra vinaigrette in a bowl on the side.

NOTE The potato salad can be chilled after it has cooled. Chill the salmon separately. When ready to serve, assemble the platter as described above.

*C*harred Rare Hawaiian Tuna Niçoise Salad

SERVES 2 AS A MAIN COURSE

12 haricots verts or other green beans
Salt
2 new potatoes
5 tablespoons extra-virgin olive oil
1 tablespoon red wine vinegar
1 teaspoon balsamic vinegar
Freshly ground white pepper
2 impeccably fresh 5-ounce tuna steaks, cut 1½-inches thick,
    skin removed
4 cups mixed greens (any one or a combination of limestone, Bibb,
    red leaf, green leaf, or curly endive), washed and well dried
4 very thin slices Maui, Bermuda, Vidalia, or any other mild onion
¼ cup julienned red, yellow, and/or green bell pepper
1 tablespoon drained capers
8 anchovy fillets
8 small black olives, preferably niçoise or Calamata
1 large unpeeled tomato, seeded, diced, and tossed with 1 teaspoon
    balsamic vinegar, a pinch of salt, and a pinch of pepper

    1. Prepare an ice bath. Bring 2 cups water to a boil with a pinch of salt. Blanch the haricots verts or green beans for 30 seconds. Drain and immediately plunge into the ice bath to stop cooking and preserve the color. Drain and set aside.

    2. Place the potatoes in a small pot and cover with water. Bring to a boil and cook, uncovered, for 15 minutes. Drain, run under cold water, and set aside.

    3. Whisk together 4 tablespoons olive oil, the red wine vinegar, and balsamic vinegar. Season to taste with salt and white pepper. Set aside.

4. Place the remaining 1 tablespoon olive oil on a plate and dip the tuna steaks in it, coating all sides. Let the tuna sit while preparing the rest of the salad.

5. Whisk the vinaigrette well and mix two-thirds of it with the salad greens. Divide the greens between 2 large plates.

6. In the same bowl, mix together the Maui onions, haricots verts or green beans, julienned pepper, and capers with the rest of the vinaigrette. Place this mixture on top of the greens, dividing it evenly.

7. Garnish each plate with 1 boiled potato, cut in half, 4 anchovy fillets, 4 olives, and half the marinated tomato.

8. Heat a cast-iron skillet extremely hot. It will take several minutes over high heat to heat the pan sufficiently. Season the tuna with salt and white pepper.

9. Place the olive oil–coated tuna in the very hot, *dry* skillet and sear it for 1 minute on each side and 10 seconds on each edge.

10. Place the tuna steaks on the greens and serve immediately.

Poultry

The rich flavors of poultry and game birds invite the use of a variety of oils, vinegars, fruits, and herbs.

Cobb Salad

Smoked Chicken, Pear, and Walnut Salad with Gorgonzola

Barbecued Duck Salad with Frisée, Jicama, Corn, and Cilantro Vinaigrette

Duck Foie Gras, French Green Beans, and Tomato

Curly Endive with Duck Liver Croutons and Cracklings

Chicken, Snow Peas, and Roasted Pepper Salad

Chicken Paillards and Papaya with Chili-Lime Vinaigrette

Egg Salad

Chinese Chicken Salad

Curried Chicken-Cantaloupe Salad

Japanese Chicken Salad

Grilled Chicken Salad with Pecans and Honey-Mustard Vinaigrette

Chicken Salad

Roasted Squab Salad with Bacon and Onions

Warm Duck Breast Salad with Grapes, Mushrooms, and Port Glaze

Warm Duck Breast Salad with Soy-Ginger Glaze, Scallions, and Shiitake Mushrooms

Warm Spinach Salad with Chicken Livers, Bacon, and Poached Egg

Warm Quail Salad with Mixed
   Greens, Sautéed Potatoes,
   Marinated Tomatoes,
   Bermuda Onions, and Red
   Wine Sauce

72 Market Street Chicken Salad

Grilled Chicken Salad with
   Chutney Mayonnaise

Cobb Salad

SERVES 4 TO 6 AS A MAIN COURSE

1 tablespoon freshly squeezed lemon juice
2 tablespoons wine vinegar
1 tablespoon Dijon mustard
6 tablespoons peanut oil or olive oil (do not use a heavy
   extra-virgin olive oil)
Salt
Freshly ground black pepper
4 cups 1-inch pieces of romaine
4 cups loosely packed watercress leaves, stems removed
1 ripe avocado, skin and pit removed, cut into ½-inch cubes
4 slices crisply cooked bacon, fat blotted off, crumbled
⅓ cup finely crumbled blue cheese or Roquefort
1 cup diced cooked turkey breast
½ cup diced seeded tomato

1. Make the vinaigrette by whisking together the lemon juice, vinegar, and mustard. Slowly whisk in the oil. Season with salt and pepper to taste.

2. In a large mixing bowl, toss together the romaine, watercress, avocado, bacon, blue cheese, turkey, and tomato.

3. Add the vinaigrette and toss. Serve at once.

Smoked Chicken, Pear, and Walnut Salad with Gorgonzola

SERVES 2 AS A MAIN COURSE

⅓ cup walnut halves (about 1 ounce) preferably freshly shelled
2 tablespoons balsamic vinegar
1 tablespoon freshly squeezed lemon juice
1 tablespoon Dijon mustard
¼ teaspoon minced garlic
Salt
Freshly ground black pepper
6 tablespoons walnut oil
1 head Belgian endive
½ small head radicchio
1 cup loosely packed watercress leaves, large stems removed
1 head limestone lettuce
1 ripe Bosc, Bartlett, or Comice pear
1 cup julienned skinned smoked chicken breast (about 6 ounces)
⅓ cup crumbled Gorgonzola or other similar blue cheese, such as Roquefort or Iowa Maytag blue

1. Preheat oven to 375° F. Place the walnut halves on a baking sheet and bake until they appear toasted, about 5 minutes. Remove from oven, let cool, and coarsely chop. Reserve.

2. In a mixing bowl, whisk together the balsamic vinegar, lemon juice, mustard, and garlic. Season with salt and pepper. Whisk in the walnut oil and set aside.

3. Slice the endive in half lengthwise. Remove the base. Cut the halves crosswise into ½-inch pieces. Place in a salad bowl.

4. Remove the core from the radicchio half and cut the leaves into bite-size strips; add to the bowl with the endive.

5. Wash and dry the watercress. Add to the bowl.

6. Remove the core from the limestone lettuce. Tear the leaves into small pieces. Wash and dry. Add to the bowl.

7. Cut the pear in half lengthwise. Remove its core and any fibers coming down from the stem. Slice the halves thinly, and add them to the bowl.

8. Add the chopped walnuts and the julienned smoked chicken to the bowl.

9. Add the vinaigrette and toss well.

10. Sprinkle the crumbled Gorgonzola on top and serve at once.

ℬarbecued Duck Salad with Frisée, Jicama, Corn, and Cilantro Vinaigrette

SERVES 4 AS A FIRST COURSE

This recipe is a creation of Jere Anderson, formerly the chef de cuisine at 72 Market Street. The flavors are very strong, but the duck and the frisée stand up perfectly well to them, and the combination of tastes is unusual and appetizing. This recipe combines several basic recipes, and is therefore rather involved. However, virtually everything can be prepared up to 3 days in advance, and the salad takes only a few minutes to assemble before serving.

4 duck legs and thighs, from ducks weighing 6 to 7 pounds (see How to Bone a Duck, page 258)

Salt

Freshly ground white pepper

¾ cup fresh or frozen corn kernels

1 teaspoon peanut oil

1 cup Chinese Barbecue Sauce (page 240)

2 heads frisée (curly endive), preferably small and pale, trimmed, washed, and dried (about 4 cups)

¼ cup diced peeled jicama (¼-inch dice)

½ cup Cilantro Vinaigrette (page 244)

1. Preheat the oven to 400° F. Season the duck legs and thighs on both sides with salt and white pepper. Place them skin side up in a baking pan. Add water up to the skin (about ½ inch), but not covering it. Bake for 1½ hours. If the water evaporates, add more, but do not submerge the skin. Cooking the legs and thighs by this method allows them to cook long enough to become tender, but not tough or dry. Keeping the skin above the water allows it to crisp, making it all the more delectable. When done, remove legs

and thighs to a platter to cool. This step can be done up to 3 days in advance, because the cooked duck legs and thighs refrigerate well. When ready to make the salad, go on to the next step.

2. Prepare an ice bath. Bring 2 cups water and a pinch of salt to a boil. Blanch the corn kernels for 30 seconds. Drain and plunge them immediately in the ice water to stop the cooking. Drain and set aside.

3. Remove the meat from the duck legs and thighs and cut it into ½-inch cubes. Heat a saucepan over moderate heat. Add the peanut oil, then the duck pieces, and cook for 3 to 4 minutes, until browned. Add the barbecue sauce, bring to a boil, lower heat, and let simmer for 1 minute. Remove from the heat and set aside while finishing the salad.

4. In a mixing bowl, combine the frisée and the jicama with the cilantro vinaigrette. Divide mixture among 4 large plates, leaving room around the border.

5. Spoon the cooked duck and barbecue sauce around the border of each plate. Sprinkle the salads with the cooked corn kernels and serve at once.

NOTE Chicken legs and thighs can be substituted for duck. Cook chicken legs and thighs by broiling or roasting them. When cool, remove the meat from the bone and proceed with step 3 of the recipe.

$\mathscr{D}$uck Foie Gras, French Green Beans, and Tomato

SERVES 4 AS A FIRST COURSE

1 teaspoon Dijon mustard
2 tablespoons sherry wine vinegar
Salt
Freshly ground white pepper
5 tablespoons walnut oil or hazelnut oil
½ pound haricots verts (if unavailable, use the finest Kentucky green beans you can find)
4 medium tomatoes
4 slices fresh duck foie gras (do not use canned) ½-inch thick (about 2 ounces each)
4 tablespoons flour

1. Whisk together the mustard and vinegar. Add a pinch of salt and pepper. Slowly whisk in the oil, forming an emulsion. Reserve.

2. Prepare the beans and tomatoes just as in the recipe for String Bean and Tomato Salad with Shallots and Tarragon Cream Dressing (page 84), omitting the dressing.

3. In a mixing bowl, combine the cooked beans, julienned tomatoes, and walnut oil vinaigrette. Toss well. Place mixture in mounds on individual plates.

4. Heat a nonstick skillet until very hot. Season the foie gras slices with salt and pepper. Place the flour on a plate and dredge the foie gras in it, coating well on all sides. Shake off any excess

flour. Sauté the slices for 30 seconds per side. They should be medium-rare and quite soft in the center. Using a spatula, lay a slice over each mound of beans and tomato and serve immediately.

NOTE For more texture, add ½ cup julienned Belgian endive 1 small head) to the haricots verts and tomato.

VARIATION

Omit the mustard in the dressing. Heat for 2 minutes 1 tablespoon minced shallots with the wine vinegar and oil. Cool to room temperature. Place the cooked foie gras on a bed of 4 cups washed and dressed mâche or watercress, dressed with the cooled dressing.

Curly Endive with Duck Liver Croutons and Cracklings

SERVES 2 AS A FIRST COURSE

The best curly endive is the type known as French endive, or what the French call *frisée*. Its leaves are small, curly, and white. Not to be confused with Belgian endive, frisée is grown here by specialty farmers and is available in produce markets. This salad is designed to use the by-products of a duck: the liver and some of the trimmed skin and fat.

Skin trimmings and fat from a boned duck
(see How to Bone a Duck, page 258)
Four ¼-inch-thick slices bread, from a French baguette
1 clove garlic, peeled
1 duck liver
Salt
Freshly ground black pepper
1 teaspoon minced shallots
1 tablespoon sherry vinegar
2 tablespoons nut oil, such as walnut, hazelnut, or peanut
3 cups washed, dried, and torn curly endive (1 head)

1. Preheat oven to 375° F.

2. Place the skin and fat in a small saucepan and heat over a low heat. The fat will melt and liquefy. Cook until the liquid is clear and the skin and remaining fat are golden brown. Strain into a

glass or ceramic bowl. Reserve separately the strained-out crack-lings and the rendered liquid fat.

3. Lay the sliced bread on a sheet pan. Brush with some of the melted duck fat. Place in the oven and brown lightly on both sides, 7 to 10 minutes total. Do not let the slices get brittle. Remove from the oven and rub with the garlic clove. Reserve.

4. Heat 1 tablespoon duck fat in a small sauté pan. Season the duck liver with salt and pepper. Sauté the liver until medium-rare, about 3 to 5 minutes. Remove it to a small plate. When it has cooled off a little, mash it with a fork. If it is dry, add 1 teaspoon duck fat while mashing. Spread this liver paste onto the croutons. Reserve.

5. Mince what remains of the garlic clove. In a small bowl, mix it with the shallot and sherry vinegar. Season to taste with salt and pepper. Whisk in the oil and 1 tablespoon duck fat. Let the rest of the fat cool to room temperature, then store it in a covered con-tainer in the refrigerator or freezer.

6. Chop the strained cracklings into bite-size pieces.

7. Toss the endive with the cracklings and the vinaigrette. Add a splash more vinegar, if necessary.

8. Place on plates and garnish with the liver croutons. Serve at once.

Chicken, Snow Peas, and Roasted Pepper Salad

SERVES 2 AS A MAIN COURSE

This dish is a perfect use for leftover chicken, be it roasted, grilled, or boiled. It calls for just a few other ingredients and makes a satisfying lunch or dinner entrée.

1 red or yellow bell pepper
10 snow peas (also called China peas)
Salt
1 small head red leaf lettuce or other soft-leaved lettuce
2 tablespoons olive oil
¼ teaspoon minced garlic
2 teaspoons sherry vinegar
Freshly ground black pepper
1 cup julienned skinless, boneless cooked chicken

1. Roast the pepper by laying it over an oven flame on your stove, under a preheated broiler, or in an extremely hot cast-iron skillet. Rotate it periodically and blacken it on all sides. When done, place it in a bowl and seal the bowl well with plastic wrap, or put in paper bag and close, allowing the pepper to steam in its own heat for about 30 minutes.

2. Trim the stems from the snow peas. Prepare an ice bath. Bring 2 cups water and ¼ teaspoon salt to a boil. Blanch the snow peas for 30 seconds. Drain and plunge immediately in the ice bath to stop the cooking and preserve their color. Drain, pat dry, and reserve.

3. Remove the roasted pepper from bowl. Under running water, remove the charred skin. It will come off easily by rubbing it with your hands or using the edge of a small paring knife. Remove the stem and the seeds. Cut the pepper into ¼-inch strips and reserve.

4. Rinse and spin dry enough lettuce leaves to line your plates or platter (about 4 leaves per person should be right).

5. Make the dressing by whisking together the oil, garlic, and vinegar. Season with a pinch of salt and pepper.

6. Place the chicken, snow peas, and roasted pepper in a mixing bowl and toss with half the dressing.

7. Lay the prepared lettuce leaves on the plates or platter. Spoon a bit of dressing on them, mound the chicken mixture into the center, and serve at once.

Chicken Paillards and Papaya with Chili-Lime Vinaigrette

SERVES 4 AS A MAIN COURSE

½ jalapeño pepper, seeded and finely minced (about 1 teaspoon)

1 teaspoon minced garlic

½ teaspoon grated lime zest (from 1 lime; zest the lime before squeezing it)

2 tablespoons freshly squeezed lime juice

2 tablespoons chopped cilantro

6 tablespoons olive oil

4 chicken breast halves, skinned and boned

Salt

Freshly ground black pepper

4 cups mixed greens, such as red leaf lettuce, romaine, butter lettuce, and watercress; washed, dried, and torn into small pieces

1½ cups peeled, seeded, and diced papaya (1 medium) or mango (½-inch dice)

1. Preheat broiler or grill.

2. Make the vinaigrette: Combine the jalapeño, garlic, lime zest, lime juice, cilantro, and olive oil. Reserve.

3. Make the paillards: Place each breast between 2 pieces of wax paper or plastic wrap. Using a mallet, flatten the breasts to about ½ inch thick. Lay the pieces in a shallow baking dish and pour about 4 tablespoons vinaigrette over them. Turn to coat them well on both sides. Do not let them marinate for more than 30 minutes or the lime juice will "cook" and dry the chicken.

4. Season the paillards with a pinch of salt and pepper. Cook the chicken for about 3 minutes per side, until cooked through but not browned. Remove to a platter.

5. Season the remaining vinaigrette with a pinch of salt and pepper. In a mixing bowl, toss the greens with the papaya or mango. Add the vinaigrette and mix well. Distribute salad among 4 large plates. Lay a cooked paillard on each salad and serve immediately.

$\mathcal{E}$gg Salad

MAKES 2 CUPS, ENOUGH FOR 4 SANDWICHES

6 large eggs
1 cup diced celery (¼-inch dice)
1 tablespoon minced scallion (white part)
1 tablespoon minced scallion (green part)
3 to 4 tablespoons mayonnaise, depending on desired consistency
Salt
Freshly ground white pepper

1. Bring 1 quart water to a boil. Using a spoon, gently lower the eggs into the water and reduce heat to a simmer. Cook for 12 minutes. Drain and cool the eggs under cold running water. Peel them as soon as they are cool enough to handle.

2. Grate or chop the eggs coarsely and place in a mixing bowl.

3. Add the celery, minced scallion (both white and green parts), and mayonnaise. Stir well. Season with salt and white pepper to taste.

4. Chill well before serving.

Chinese Chicken Salad

SERVES 4 TO 6 AS A MAIN COURSE

10 wonton skins
2 cups plus 5 tablespoons peanut oil
½ cup raw unsalted cashews (about 2 ounces)
4 fresh water chestnuts (see Note)
1 small head romaine
1 small head Napa or Chinese cabbage
4 large shiitake mushroom caps, cut in ¼-inch strips
Salt
Freshly ground white pepper
3 cups shredded skinless cooked chicken (from one 3- to 4-pound
    chicken, roasted, grilled, or barbecued)
1 cup bean sprouts
¼ cup julienned scallions (white part and 1 inch of green)
¼ cup julienned Chinese preserved red ginger
2 tablespoons rice-wine vinegar
2 teaspoons soy sauce
2 tablespoons toasted sesame oil
2 tablespoons freshly squeezed lemon juice
2 teaspoons brown sugar
½ teaspoon chili oil
1 tablespoon finely minced peeled fresh ginger
½ teaspoon minced garlic
2 teaspoons hoisin sauce

1. Cut the wonton skins into ¼-inch strips and toss in a bowl to
separate. Heat 2 cups peanut oil in a shallow pan until a strip of
wonton skin blisters when dropped in. Working with one-third of
the skins at a time, fry the strips until golden, about 1 minute.
Remove each batch with a skimmer and drain on several layers of
paper towels. This may be done a few hours ahead of time.

2. Heat the oven to 375° F. Spread the cashews on a baking sheet and toast lightly, about 5 minutes. Remove from the oven and cool. Chop coarsely and set aside.

3. Peel the water chestnuts with a paring knife, removing all black specks and rinsing often under cold running water. Chop into ¼-inch dice. Reserve in a bowl of water, refrigerated.

4. Remove the outer dark green leaves of the romaine, as well as the dark tops of the remaining leaves. Cut the lighter leaves crosswise into 1-inch strips. Wash and dry thoroughly. You should have about 3 cups. Do the same with the cabbage. Place the greens in a large mixing or salad bowl.

5. Heat 1 tablespoon peanut oil in a small frying pan. Season the shiitakes with a pinch of salt and white pepper, then sauté just until limp. Remove from the pan and cool.

6. To the greens add the chicken, bean sprouts, scallions, preserved ginger, cashews, and shiitakes. Toss well.

7. In a separate bowl, whisk together the rice-wine vinegar, soy sauce, sesame oil, lemon juice, brown sugar, chili oil, fresh ginger, garlic, and hoisin. Season with a pinch of salt and white pepper (be careful, as the soy sauce is already salty). Slowly whisk in the remaining 4 tablespoons peanut oil.

8. Drain the water chestnuts and add to the salad bowl. Pour the dressing over the salad and toss well. Divide between serving plates or serve in a salad bowl. Top with the fried wonton skins.

NOTE Fresh water chestnuts bear no resemblance to those found in a can. They have a thin, tough skin, which can be cut away to reveal a delightful, sweet interior, much like a very dense jicama. If you can't find them, don't substitute canned. Once peeled, fresh water chestnuts can be kept refrigerated for several hours if submerged in water.

Curried Chicken-Cantaloupe Salad

SERVES 2 AS A MAIN COURSE; 4 AS AN APPETIZER

This is a variation of a recipe given to me by one of my partners, Margo Barbakow. She has always been a salad lover, and has encouraged the experimentation necessary for this book.

½ cup low-sodium chicken broth
1 teaspoon curry powder
1 small cantaloupe
1 cup cubed cooked chicken, preferably white meat, all skin and fat removed
½ cup seedless green grapes, halved
½ cup diced celery
2 tablespoons toasted slivered almonds
½ cup mayonnaise
½ cup sour cream
1 teaspoon soy sauce
1 tablespoon freshly squeezed lemon juice
Salt
Freshly ground white pepper
8 large leaves of a flat variety of lettuce, such as red leaf

1. In a small saucepan, combine the chicken broth and curry powder. Bring to a boil and reduce until you have about 3 tablespoons of syrup. Cool to room temperature.

2. Cut the cantaloupe in half and remove the seeds. Cut each half into 1-inch wedges and cut away the rind. Cut each wedge into ½-inch cubes.

3. In a mixing bowl, combine the melon, chicken, grapes, celery, almonds.

4. In a separate bowl, whisk together the mayonnaise and reduced curry syrup. Add the sour cream, soy sauce, and lemon juice. Add salt and pepper, if necessary.

5. Add the dressing to the melon-chicken mixture and toss to combine well. Serve on lettuce leaves.

Japanese Chicken Salad

This salad, one of my favorites, works well as a first course, light lunch, main course, or on a buffet table. If preparing the ingredients in advance, keep them separate. Combine and add the vinaigrette just before serving.

10 snow pea pods
2 cups julienned roasted or boiled chicken, skin and fat removed, preferably white meat (2 breast halves from a 3½- to 4-pound chicken)
1 cup washed and dried watercress leaves, thick stems removed
2 cups ½-inch-pieces Belgian endive (two 3-ounce heads)
¼ cup 2-inch julienned carrot
¼ cup 2-inch julienned celery
¼ cup 2-inch julienned cucumber (preferably unpeeled European hothouse variety; if you use the regular type, peel and seed)
¼ cup 2-inch julienned peeled daikon root
¼ cup daikon sprouts, cut in 2-inch lengths
½ cup bean sprouts
2 tablespoons minced chives
½ cup Japanese Vinaigrette (page 245)

1. Prepare an ice bath. Blanch the snow peas in 2 cups boiling water with ¼ teaspoon salt added for 30 seconds. Drain and plunge immediately into the ice bath. Drain and cut the pods lengthwise into fine julienne strips.

2. Mix all of the ingredients, except the Japanese vinaigrette, together in a large mixing bowl. Toss well.

3. Add the vinaigrette and toss again. Serve at once.

VARIATIONS

1. Japanese Chicken Salad with Grilled Chicken Breast

Marinate 2 large chicken breasts (with or without the skin) in 4 tablespoons Japanese vinaigrette for at least 2 hours, or up to 8, refrigerated. Preheat a grill or broiler and cook the chicken until just done. Cool slightly and slice the chicken breasts on a diagonal. Toss the salad ingredients with 6 to 7 tablespoons Japanese vinaigrette and mound it on plates. Surround the salads with the sliced chicken breasts. Top each slice with a few drops of Japanese vinaigrette. Serve at once.

2. Grilled Shrimp Salad with Japanese Vinaigrette

Omit the chicken from the main recipe. Marinate 12 ounces large shrimp (16 to 20 per pound), which have been shelled and deveined, in 4 tablespoons Japanese vinaigrette. Prepare all of the salad ingredients. Preheat your grill or broiler, and cook the shrimp until they are just pink; do not overcook. Combine the salad ingredients with 6 to 7 tablespoons Japanese vinaigrette, toss well, and mound the salad on individual plates. Surround the salads with the grilled (or broiled) shrimp and top each shrimp with a few additional drops of vinaigrette. Serve at once.

*G*rilled Chicken Salad with Pecans and Honey-Mustard Vinaigrette

SERVES 4 AS A LIGHT MAIN COURSE

⅓ cup pecan halves (about 1 ounce)
½ teaspoon sugar
⅛ teaspoon cayenne
1 tablespoon minced shallots
4 tablespoons honey vinegar or sherry vinegar
1 tablespoon honey
1 tablespoon Dijon mustard
1 tablespoon coarse-grained mustard
1 teaspoon soy sauce
6 tablespoons walnut oil or peanut oil
Freshly ground black pepper
4 chicken breast halves, skinned and boned
4 large shiitake mushroom caps (about 3 inches in diameter)
1 cup watercress leaves, washed and dried, large stems removed
2 cups red leaf lettuce pieces, washed and dried
2 cups Bibb lettuce washed and dried
¼ cup julienned peeled carrot

1. Preheat oven to 375° F. Place the pecans on a baking sheet and toast in the oven until crisp, 10 to 12 minutes. Remove from the oven and toss in a bowl with the sugar and cayenne. Reserve. Turn the oven to broil or heat a grill.

2. Place the shallots in a small saucepan with the vinegar. Reduce over high heat by half. Remove from heat and stir in the honey. When cool, place in a mixing bowl. Whisk in the mustards, soy sauce, and oil. Season to taste with pepper. Reserve.

3. Spoon half the vinaigrette over the chicken breasts and turn them around in it to coat. Grill or broil until just done. At the same time, grill or broil the mushroom caps. When done, cut the mushrooms into ¼-inch strips.

4. Toss the greens, carrot, and mushrooms with the balance of the vinaigrette. Place on 4 individual plates, and lay a breast over each. Distribute the pecans around each plate and serve at once.

Chicken Salad

MAKES 4½ TO 5 CUPS

One 3- to 4-pound cooked chicken, skin and fat removed, meat diced
   (3½ to 4 cups meat in ½-inch dice)
1 cup diced celery
1 teaspoon chopped fresh tarragon or parsley
1 teaspoon freshly squeezed lemon juice
½ cup mayonnaise
1 tablespoon Dijon mustard
1 tablespoon coarse-grained mustard
Salt
Freshly ground black pepper

1. Place the diced chicken and celery in a mixing bowl.

2. In a separate mixing bowl, whisk together the tarragon, lemon juice, mayonnaise, and both mustards. Season with salt and pepper.

3. Pour the dressing over the chicken and celery and fold thoroughly. This can be served at once but benefits from sitting in the refrigerator for several hours before serving.

$\mathscr{R}$oast Squab Salad with Bacon and Onions

SERVES 4 AS A FIRST COURSE; 2 AS A MAIN COURSE

Squab has a deep, gamey flavor. I pair it with other strong flavors, such as the bacon, onion, and rosemary (or thyme) in this recipe.

¼ pound smoked slab bacon, rind removed, cut into ½-inch dice (about ¾ cup)

2 whole squabs (approximately 14 ounces each)

Salt

Freshly ground black pepper

2 sprigs fresh rosemary or thyme

2 large cloves garlic, peeled

16 pearl or very small boiling onions (not more than 1 inch in diameter), peeled

2 tablespoons light olive oil

1 cup ½-inch French bread cubes (from about 2 slices of old bread or 1 small roll)

2 tablespoons balsamic vinegar

2 tablespoons extra-virgin olive oil

4 cups mesclun or mixed greens, including curly endive, radicchio, Belgian endive, arugula, or red leaf lettuce, washed and dried

1. Preheat oven to 450° F.

2. Bring 1 quart water to a boil. Blanch the bacon for 5 minutes. Drain and rinse under cold running water. Reserve.

3. Season the skin and cavities of the squabs with salt and pepper. Put 1 sprig of rosemary or thyme in the large cavity of each bird. Tuck the wings under the body. Place the birds, breast down, in a low-sided baking dish or ovenproof sauté pan. Add 1 clove garlic, the onions, and the blanched bacon to the pan. Bake for 30 to 35 minutes, basting the birds and turning the onions every

10 minutes, until the juices run clear when a small knife is inserted into a thigh.

4. While the birds are roasting, make the croutons. Heat the light olive oil in a frying pan. Slice the remaining clove of garlic and sauté until lightly browned, about 3 minutes. Remove the garlic with a slotted spoon. Add the cubed bread and cook, tossing frequently, until golden brown on all sides. Remove the croutons with a slotted spoon and drain on several layers of paper towels. Reserve.

5. When the squabs are done, remove them to a plate and let sit for 10 minutes. Discard the garlic clove from the pan. Using a slotted spoon, remove the bacon and onions and reserve. Place the pan on a slight angle to let the juices collect to one side.

6. After a few minutes, skim the grease from the pan. Add the vinegar to the remaining liquid and scrape the caramelized juices adhering to the pan into the vinegar. Transfer to a bowl and whisk in the extra-virgin olive oil, a pinch of pepper, and any juices that have collected in the cavities of the squabs or in the plate beneath them. Whisk well.

7. Discard the herbs in the birds. Using a small sharp knife, cut the legs and thighs away from the bodies. Cut away the wings and reserve for a stock. Cut through on either side of the breastbone, back through to the wishbone, and lift the breasts away from the rib cage. Cut the breasts, against the grain, into thin slices. Reserve the wings and carcasses for a stock (they may be frozen).

8. In a mixing bowl, toss the greens with the croutons. Pour in half the vinaigrette and toss again. Place the salad on individual plates. Place the onions and bacon in a circle around the salad. Lay 1 sliced breast and 1 leg and thigh on each salad for a first course, 2 of each for a main course. Top the meat with the remaining vinaigrette. Serve at once.

$\mathscr{W}$arm Duck Breast Salad with Grapes, Mushrooms, and Port Glaze

SERVES 2

FOR THE PORT GLAZE

2 tablespoons butter

2 tablespoons finely minced shallots

2 tablespoons minced shiitake mushroom stems

1 sprig tarragon, chopped into several pieces

1 tablespoon red wine vinegar

½ cup port

½ cup duck, veal, or chicken stock, or canned low-sodium
   chicken broth

FOR THE VINAIGRETTE

1 tablespoon red wine vinegar

½ teaspoon Dijon mustard

3 tablespoons peanut oil or vegetable oil

Salt

Freshly ground white pepper

FOR THE SALAD

Two 6-ounce duck breasts (from 6- to 7-pound duck; see How to Bone
   a Duck, page 258)

½ cup quartered shiitake mushroom caps

2 cups loosely packed watercress leaves

2 cups sliced Belgian endive (from 2 endives, 4 to 5 inches long)

¼ cup red seedless grapes, quartered lengthwise

1. Preheat the oven to 150° F. Begin the port glaze by melting 1 tablespoon butter in a small saucepan. Add the shallots, mushroom stems, and tarragon. Cook over moderate heat until the shallots and mushrooms begin to brown. Add the red wine vinegar and

the port. Reduce by half. Add the stock and reduce by one-half to two-thirds, until the sauce thickly coats a spoon. Remove from heat and whisk in 1 tablespoon butter. Strain. Keep warm over very low heat while preparing the rest of the salad.

2. While the sauce is reducing, make the vinaigrette. In a small bowl, whisk together the red wine vinegar and the Dijon mustard. Slowly whisk in the oil, to create an emulsion. Season to taste with salt and white pepper. Reserve.

3. Score the skin of the duck breasts, taking care to not cut into the meat. Season both sides with salt and white pepper. Heat a small frying pan over moderate heat and place the duck breasts, skin side down and without oil, in the pan. Cook the breasts for 10 to 12 minutes, keeping them skin side down for most of that time. They should be medium-rare. When done, remove them from the pan, place on a plate, and keep warm in the oven. Discard all but 1 tablespoon of fat and sauté the quartered shiitake mushroom caps until lightly cooked, about 1 minute. Season to taste with salt and white pepper. Remove from the pan and keep warm in the oven.

4. Mix the watercress and endive with the vinaigrette and divide the salad between 2 large dinner plates. Place equal amounts of sautéed mushrooms on top of each mound of salad. Slice the duck breasts thinly on a diagonal, and arrange the slices on the plates around the mounds of greens. Coat each slice of duck with the warm port glaze. Sprinkle the grape quarters over the sauced slices of duck, and serve at once.

Warm Duck Breast Salad with Soy-Ginger Glaze, Scallions, and Shiitake Mushrooms

SERVES 4

This salad works best as an entrée, at lunch or dinner.

3 tablespoons olive oil

6 tablespoons peanut oil

2 tablespoons plus 1 teaspoon freshly squeezed lemon juice

2½ tablespoons soy sauce

Freshly ground white pepper

3 tablespoons minced peeled fresh ginger

½ cup coarsely chopped scallions (equal amount of green and white parts)

Shiitake mushroom stems

½ teaspoon minced garlic

½ cup rice-wine vinegar

1 cup duck, veal, or chicken stock, or canned low-sodium chicken broth

2 tablespoons mirin (sweet cooking sake; optional)

Four 6- to 7-ounce duck breasts (from ducks weighing 6 to 7 pounds) or two 6-pound ducks (see How to Bone a Duck, page 258)

Salt

½ cup julienned scallions (equal amounts of green and white parts)

½ cup julienned shiitake mushroom caps (four 2-inch-diameter mushrooms)

6 to 8 cups mixed greens, such as white curly endive, watercress, red leaf lettuce, and Belgian endive, washed and dried

1. Prepare the soy vinaigrette by whisking together the olive oil, 3 tablespoons peanut oil, lemon juice, 1½ tablespoons soy sauce, and a pinch of white pepper. Add 1 tablespoon ginger and set aside.

2. In a saucepan, sweat the chopped scallions (not the julienned ones), chopped mushroom stems, remaining 2 tablespoons ginger, and the garlic in 2 tablespoons peanut oil until soft. Deglaze with the rice-wine vinegar and reduce by half. Add the stock and, if desired, the mirin. Reduce by one-half to two-thirds, or until the sauce thickly coats a spoon. Remove from the heat and stir in the remaining soy sauce to taste. Strain through a fine-mesh sieve. Keep warm over very low heat.

3. Preheat oven to 150° F. Score the skin of the duck breasts, taking care to not cut through to the meat, and season both sides with salt and white pepper. Either grill them or sauté in a very hot dry pan, skin side down most of the time, over medium-high heat. When the skin is nicely crisped and the breasts are almost medium-rare (after about 8 minutes), drain off the grease and turn the breasts over. Cook for an additional 1 or 2 minutes and remove from the heat. Do not overcook; they should be cooked no more than medium-rare. Keep warm in the oven.

4. In a sauté pan over high heat, sauté the julienned scallions with the julienned shiitake mushroom caps in remaining 1 table-spoon peanut oil. Cook lightly and season with salt and white pepper.

5. Slice the duck breasts on the diagonal, making about 6 slices per breast. Pour any juices from the duck into the sauce.

6. Stir the soy vinaigrette and toss it with the greens. Divide the greens among 4 large plates, mounding them in the center.

7. Lay the slices of duck in a circle around the mounds of greens, using 1 breast per plate.

8. Top each slice of duck with some of the warm glaze.

9. Spoon some of the sautéed scallions and mushrooms on top of each salad. Serve at once.

$\mathcal{W}$arm Spinach Salad with Chicken Livers, Bacon, and Poached Egg

SERVES 2 AS A MAIN COURSE

4 cups spinach leaves, cleaned and well dried
¼ pound smoked slab bacon, rind removed, or 4 thick slices, trimmed
¼ pound chicken livers
Salt
3 tablespoons sherry vinegar
Freshly ground black pepper
2 tablespoons julienned cornichons
1 tablespoon minced shallots
2 packed tablespoons brown sugar
2 large eggs

1. Place the spinach in a large mixing bowl and reserve.

2. Cut the slab bacon into ¼-inch thick slices. Cut across each slice to make strips approximately ¼-inch by ¼-inch by 1-inch long. Dice the bacon slices. You should have about ¾ cup. Reserve.

3. Trim the chicken livers of all fat and gristle. Separate the 2 lobes of each liver and cut each lobe into 2 pieces. Reserve.

4. Bring 1 quart water to a boil with 1 teaspoon salt and 1 tablespoon vinegar in a shallow saucepan (or set up an egg poacher, if available).

5. Heat a frying pan until quite hot and cook the bacon until it starts to turn brown. Reduce heat and add the chicken livers. Season *lightly* with salt (the bacon is already salty) and pepper. Cook for a few minutes, occasionally turning the livers. When they are

nicely browned but still soft, add the cornichons and shallots. Stir and continue cooking for a moment, but do not let the shallots burn.

6. Add the brown sugar and the rest of the vinegar. Stir again. As soon as the sugar has melted, remove the pan from the heat. Keep this mixture warm by simply leaving it in the saucepan off the heat.

7. Reduce boiling water to a simmer and, with a whisk, stir the water to create a funnel. Gently break 1 egg into a small bowl and set it into the center of the funnel, then immediately do the same with the other egg, while the water is still spinning. Alternatively, poach the eggs in an egg poacher. Let them simmer for about 4 minutes, until the white solidifies around the yolk, but the yolk remains soft. Once the eggs are poached, the salad is ready for assembly.

8. Pour the bacon and chicken liver mixture over the spinach and toss well. The spinach will wilt slightly. Place the spinach on a serving platter or divide between 2 individual plates.

9. Top with the poached eggs and serve immediately.

Warm Quail Salad with Mixed Greens, Sautéed Potatoes, Marinated Tomatoes, Bermuda Onion, and Red Wine Sauce

SERVES 4

This is a composed salad of greens mixed with a vinaigrette, sautéed diced potatoes, and sautéed Bermuda onions. It is garnished with diced tomato that has been marinated with balsamic vinegar and a sautéed boneless quail. The quail is topped with a Bordelaise-style red wine sauce just before serving to add richness and complexity to the flavors of the salad.

The recipe for the Bordelaise sauce will make more than you need for this salad; I suggest freezing the rest, as it makes an excellent accompaniment for beef, lamb, game, or veal.

4 "glove-boned" quail
6 tablespoons extra-virgin olive oil
1 clove garlic, thinly sliced
1 sprig fresh rosemary or tarragon
Freshly ground black pepper
½ cup diced unpeeled seeded tomato
Salt
1 teaspoon balsamic vinegar
2 tablespoons red wine vinegar
1 teaspoon Dijon mustard
½ cup Red Wine Sauce or Bordelaise (page 241)
½ cup diced peeled parboiled new potatoes (4 to 5)
½ cup thinly sliced Bermuda onion (1 small)
4 cups assorted mixed greens, washed, dried, and chilled; "baby" or young lettuces are preferable, along with arugula, radicchio, Belgian endive, and/or watercress.

1. Marinate the quail in 1 tablespoon olive oil, the garlic, tarragon or rosemary, and a pinch of freshly ground pepper. Refrigerate until ready to use, for 2 to 48 hours.

2. Sprinkle the tomato with salt and pepper and add the balsamic vinegar. Refrigerate.

3. Make a vinaigrette by whisking together the red wine vinegar, Dijon mustard, and 4 tablespoons olive oil, added slowly. Season with salt and pepper and set aside.

Steps 1–3 can be done up to a day in advance. The following steps should be done just before serving the salad.

4. Heat the red wine sauce and keep warm over very low heat.

5. Heat oven to 150° F. Season the quail with a pinch of salt (they already have pepper). Heat a sauté pan until very hot. Add the remaining 1 tablespoon olive oil and cook the quail until golden brown on all sides, 7 to 10 minutes total. Do not overcook because they are very small and will dry out easily. When done, remove from the pan and place in the oven to keep warm.

6. Drain and pat dry the parboiled potatoes, and add them to the hot pan along with the onion. Sauté until the potatoes start to brown; the onions will still be crunchy. Remove the pan from the heat but leave the potatoes and onion in the pan for a moment.

7. Mix the chilled greens with the warm potato-onion mixture. Toss with the vinaigrette.

8. Divide this mixture among 4 salad plates. Sprinkle the marinated tomatoes around the border of each plate. Place 1 warm quail on each salad, and top with red wine sauce. Serve at once.

72 Market Street Chicken Salad

SERVES 4 AS A MAIN COURSE

2 tablespoons pine nuts

8 cups mixed salad greens, washed and dried (red leaf, green leaf, and Bibb work well)

1½ cups julienned cooked chicken, skin removed (preferably roasted or grilled)

¼ cup julienned drained sun-dried tomatoes, packed in oil

½ cup diced tomato (1 small)

4 tablespoons extra-virgin olive oil

2 tablespoons balsamic vinegar

2 tablespoons red wine vinegar

Salt

Freshly ground black pepper

½ recipe Roasted Peppers with Garlic and Extra-Virgin Olive Oil (page 38)

2 ounces soft goat cheese, such as Montrachet

1. Heat the oven to 350° F. Toast the pine nuts on a baking sheet for 5 minutes, or until lightly browned. Let them cool to room temperature.

2. In a large mixing bowl, toss the greens with the chicken, sun-dried tomatoes, fresh tomato, and pine nuts.

3. Whisk together the oil and both vinegars. Season to taste with salt and pepper.

4. Add the dressing to the mixing bowl (if you prefer your salad lightly dressed, add a little at a time, as desired).

5. Transfer the salad to a serving bowl or platter. Lay the strips of roasted pepper on the salad. Crumble the goat cheese over the salad and serve at once.

Grilled Chicken Salad with Chutney Mayonnaise

MAKES 2 PINTS, ENOUGH FOR 6 TO 8 SERVINGS

4 boneless, skinless chicken breast halves
1¼ cups Garlic-Herb Marinade for Grilling (page 251)
Salt
Freshly ground black pepper
½ cup chopped celery
¼ cup mayonnaise or additional yogurt
½ cup chutney (see Note)
¼ cup plain yogurt

1. Marinate the chicken breasts overnight, refrigerated, in the garlic-herb marinade. Turn occasionally.

2. Preheat your grill or broiler. Remove the chicken from the marinade and drain, but do not scrape off the excess marinade. Sprinkle lightly with salt and pepper. Grill or broil on both sides until cooked through. Cool until the chicken can be handled. Cut into ½-inch cubes.

3. Combine the chicken and celery in a bowl.

4. In a separate bowl, stir together the mayonnaise, chutney, and yogurt. Add dressing to the chicken and mix to combine thoroughly with a rubber spatula. Chill for at least 2 hours before serving.

NOTE Use a chutney that combines tart, spicy, and sweet flavors, such as apple-raisin. If the chutney is very chunky, chop it before combining it with the other ingredients.

Meats

Combining meats with salad greens provides an opportunity to use leftover meats in a second meal. It also allows you to create composed salads that make a filling meal out of a small amount of meat.

Veal Sweetbread Salad with Potatoes and Hazelnut Vinaigrette

Chef's Salad

Italian Chef's Salad

Meat Salad with Green Beans, Beets, and Horseradish

Lamb Salad with Roasted Artichoke and Goat Cheese

Steak and Arugula Salad

Smoked Ham, Belgian Endive, Watercress, and Hearts of Palm Salad

Veal Sweetbread Salad with Potatoes and Hazelnut Vinaigrette

SERVES 4 AS A FIRST COURSE

12 ounces veal sweetbreads (2 pair)
Salt
8 new potatoes
2 shallots, minced
8 tablespoons hazelnut oil
4 tablespoons peanut oil
4 tablespoons sherry vinegar
Freshly ground black pepper
2 tablespoons clarified butter
2 tablespoons flour
4 cups mixed greens, such as watercress, Belgian endive, Bibb lettuce, red leaf, and/or frisée, washed and dried
1 tablespoon minced chives

1. Separate the lobes of the sweetbreads and soak them in cold water for at least 4 hours and as long as 24 hours. Change the water several times. Keep refrigerated.

2. One hour before serving, drain the sweetbreads and place them in a pot with 2 quarts cold fresh water and 2 teaspoons salt. Bring slowly to a boil. As soon as the water boils, remove the sweetbreads and rinse them under cold water to stop the cooking.

Place the sweetbreads on a plate, place another plate on top, and refrigerate for 1 hour to squeeze out any remaining water and keep the sweetbreads firm. Peel the thin membranes and slice the lobes into ⅓-inch pieces.

3. Meanwhile, wash the potatoes and cook them, unpeeled, in boiling salted water, until a knife pierces them easily but doesn't break them apart, about 15 minutes. Drain and cut them, still unpeeled, into ⅓-inch-thick slices.

4. Prepare the vinaigrette by whisking together the shallots, oils, and sherry vinegar. Season to taste with salt and pepper.

5. Heat 1 tablespoon clarified butter in a frying pan. Season the sweetbreads with salt and pepper. Dredge the pieces of sweetbread in the flour, shake off any excess, and fry them quickly, about 30 seconds per side, in the hot butter. Drain on paper towels, place on a plate, and brush each piece with a bit of vinaigrette.

6. Heat the remaining clarified butter in the same frying pan. Sauté the potatoes quickly, just until lightly browned. Drain on paper towels. Season with salt and pepper.

7. Toss the greens with the remaining vinaigrette, and divide among 4 plates. Distribute the sweetbreads and potatoes among the 4 salads and sprinkle with chives. Serve at once.

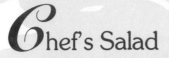

Chef's Salad

SERVES 4 AS A MAIN COURSE

After many years of food trends, this salad remains a lunchtime favorite. I suggest using a variety of greens and not loading the salad down with too much meat and cheese, as is often done. Also, a vinaigrette with Dijon mustard works best because it doesn't mask the flavors of the meats and cheese. Of course, the salad can be served with Thousand Island Dressing (page 249) or Creamy Blue Cheese Dressing (page 246). If using blue cheese dressing, omit the Swiss cheese in the salad; it does not make much sense to garnish one with the other. A second type of ham, or roast beef, could be substituted for the cheese.

1 head romaine lettuce
1 small head radicchio
1 cup watercress leaves, large stems removed, washed and spun dry
2 tablespoons red wine vinegar
1 tablespoon Dijon mustard
Salt
Freshly ground black pepper
6 tablespoons olive oil or peanut oil
1 cup julienned smoked or baked ham (4 ounces)
1 cup julienned turkey or chicken breast (4 ounces) (avoid using
    processed turkey—it is better to omit it entirely)
1 cup julienned Swiss cheese or Gruyère (5 ounces)
2 hard-boiled eggs, each cut into 4 wedges
2 medium tomatoes, stems removed, each cut into 6 to 8 wedges

1. Remove and discard the large dark green outer leaves of romaine. Cut off and discard the green tops from the center leaves. Cut what remains into 1-inch-wide strips. Wash and spin dry. Place in a large serving bowl.

2. Cut the radicchio in half lengthwise. Remove and discard the core and base from each half. Cut the halves into 1-inch-wide strips, pulling apart the leaves. Add to the salad bowl.

3. Add the watercress leaves. Toss well to mix the three varieties of greens.

4. In a small bowl, whisk together the vinegar and mustard. Season to taste with salt and pepper. Whisk in the oil. Check the seasoning.

5. Toss the salad greens with the vinaigrette. In a spoke-wheel fashion, lay the julienned meats and cheese over the greens. Place the egg and tomato wedges around the outer edge of the bowl. Serve at once.

$\mathcal{I}$talian Chef's Salad

A chef's salad can be composed of any number of ingredients, as long as some cold meats, cheeses, and greens are present. Here is an example with Mediterranean roots.

2 tablespoons red wine vinegar

1 tablespoon Dijon mustard

2 teaspoons minced garlic

2 teaspoons minced anchovy (optional)

2 teaspoons Worcestershire sauce

6 tablespoons olive oil

Freshly ground black pepper

Salt (optional; use if anchovy is omitted)

2 heads romaine, or 3 heads radicchio and 3 cups arugula, washed and dried

¼ pound julienned Italian salami (about 1 cup)

¼ pound julienned mortadella (about 1 cup)

¼ pound julienned Italian provolone (about 1 cup)

½ cup shaved Italian Parmesan (about 2 ounces) (thinly sliced with a cheese plane or sharp knife, but not grated)

1 red bell pepper, seeded and julienned

1 cup drained canned or cooked chick-peas (see Marinated Chick-Peas, page 226)

2 medium tomatoes, stemmed and cut into 6 to 8 wedges each

1. Make the vinaigrette by whisking together the vinegar, mustard, garlic, anchovy (if desired), Worcestershire, and olive oil. Season with plenty of pepper and some salt if you are omitting the anchovy. The dressing will not emulsify, so it will require whisking before use. Reserve.

2. **Prepare the greens.** If using romaine, remove and discard the outer dark green leaves. Tear or cut the remaining lettuce into 2-inch pieces. You should have about 6 cups. Wash and dry well. If using radicchio, cut the heads in half lengthwise. Remove the core and base. Cut or tear the leaves into 2-inch pieces. Toss with the arugula.

3. In a large salad bowl, combine the greens with the meats, cheeses, bell peppers, and chick-peas. Toss well. Add the vinaigrette (remember to whisk it first) and toss again. You may not need to use all of the vinaigrette. Place the tomato wedges around the border of the salad, and serve at once.

Meat Salad with Green Beans, Beets, and Horseradish

SERVES 4 AS A MAIN COURSE

Here's a salad designed to make use of leftover meat. Ideally, it would be made with boiled beef, calf's tongue, or leg of lamb. Because this dish is made principally with a leftover, I am giving many substitutions or options in the recipe to accommodate what might be found in your larder.

1 pound raw beets or potatoes (2½ inches in diameter)
Salt
3 tablespoons vinegar, preferably red wine, sherry, or white tarragon vinegar
1 teaspoon Dijon or coarse-grained mustard
1 teaspoon prepared horseradish (if unavailable, omit and add another teaspoon mustard)
4 tablespoons minced shallots, yellow onion, or scallions
1 tablespoon each minced capers and cornichons, or 2 tablespoons of one or the other
1 tablespoon chopped parsley or fresh tarragon or a combination
Freshly ground black pepper
½ cup peanut oil, walnut oil, or light olive oil
3 cups trimmed julienned leftover meat (about 1 pound)
2 cups trimmed green beans or julienned celery
8 lettuce leaves, washed and dried
2 hard-boiled eggs, whites and yolks separated

1. Scrub the beets well with a vegetable brush. Place them in a pot and cover with water. Add 1 teaspoon salt. Bring to a boil, reduce heat, and simmer until tender, about 30 minutes. A paring knife should pierce them easily. Remove from the cooking liquid and cool the beets enough so they may be handled easily.

2. Meanwhile, prepare the vinaigrette by whisking together the vinegar, mustard, horseradish, shallots or onion, capers, cornichons, and herbs. Add a pinch of salt and pepper. Whisk in the oil.

3. Spoon 4 tablespoons dressing onto the meat and toss well. Let sit at room temperature until the salad is completed.

4. Prepare an ice bath. Bring 1 quart water to a boil with ½ teaspoon salt. Cook the string beans for 4 to 6 minutes (if using celery, just blanch it for 30 seconds). Drain and submerge in ice bath to stop cooking. Drain again and reserve until needed.

5. When the beets (or potatoes) are cool, peel and julienne them to roughly resemble the beef and string beans (if using potatoes, cut them into ½-inch cubes). Reserve until needed.

6. When ready to serve, lay the lettuce leaves on a serving platter. Season the beets with several tablespoons of vinaigrette and place them on top of the lettuce, spreading them out to leave a ring of lettuce around them. Season the green beans with some vinaigrette and place them on top of the beets, leaving a ring of beets seen around the edge. Do the same with the beef, leaving another concentric ring. Chop the egg whites and sprinkle them over the salad; sieve the yolks over all. Serve at once.

Lamb Salad with Roasted Artichoke and Goat Cheese

SERVES 2 AS A MAIN COURSE

2 sprigs fresh tarragon

2 cloves garlic, peeled and cut in slivers

7 tablespoons olive oil

Freshly ground black pepper

1 boneless lamb loin, or 2 lamb tenderloins (approximately 8 to 10 ounces total)

Salt

2 tablespoons freshly squeezed lemon juice

2 artichokes (8 to 9 ounces each), prepared for cooking (see Whole Artichokes with Creamy Herb Dressing, page 247)

1 medium tomato

1 tablespoon balsamic vinegar

4 ounces goat cheese, preferably Montrachet, cut into 1½-inch cubes

½ cup cubed French bread (from approximately 1 thick slice)

1 tablespoon vegetable oil

1 tablespoon red wine

1 tablespoon red wine vinegar

1 tablespoon Dijon mustard

4 cups mesclun

1. Chop the tarragon leaves coarsely. Combine them with half the garlic and 2 tablespoons olive oil. Add a generous amount of freshly ground pepper and pour over the lamb. Marinate for at least 1 hour or up to 24 hours, refrigerated.

2. Preheat the oven to 400° F. Combine 2 quarts of cold water with 1 teaspoon salt and the lemon juice. Cook the artichokes according to the directions on page 261. When cooked, remove the choke following the directions in the same recipe. Set the artichokes aside until needed. This step may be done up to 1 day in advance, in which case the artichokes should be kept refrigerated.

3. If you grill the lamb, heat the grill now. While the artichokes are cooking, cut the tomato in half horizontally. Gently squeeze out the juice and seeds and discard. Chop the tomato into ¼-inch dice. Season with salt and pepper and toss with the balsamic vinegar. Set aside.

4. Stuff the center cavity of each cooled artichoke with a 1½-inch cube of goat cheese. Place the stuffed artichokes on an oiled baking sheet and cook in oven until cheese is heated through, about 20 minutes.

5. Meanwhile, make the croutons following the directions for Caesar Salad on page 34, using 1 tablespoon olive oil, the vegetable oil, and the remaining garlic.

6. Make the vinaigrette by whisking together the red wine, red wine vinegar, and mustard. Add the remaining olive oil slowly, whisking to make an emulsion. Season with salt and pepper.

7. When the artichokes are ready, turn the oven off and leave them in the oven to keep them warm. Remove the lamb from the marinade (do not scrape) and season with a pinch of salt. If grilling, do so on all sides. If sautéing, heat a heavy cast-iron skillet until very hot. Sear the lamb on all sides using the oil clinging to it from the marinade. In either case, the lamb will be best when cooked medium-rare, so only a few minutes of cooking will be required. Let the cooked lamb rest for 5 minutes before slicing.

8. Mix the greens with the croutons and the vinaigrette. Divide between 2 large plates.

9. With a very sharp knife, slice the lamb into ¼-inch pieces, on an angle against the grain.

10. Form a well in the middle of the greens and place the stuffed artichoke in it. Sprinkle the chopped tomatoes around the artichokes. Lay the slices of lamb over the greens. Serve at once.

Steak and Arugula Salad

SERVES 2 AS A MAIN COURSE

This easy-to-fix salad can be made with leftover steak or roast beef, though it is best with warm, just-cooked meat.

4 tablespoons extra-virgin olive oil
½ teaspoon minced garlic
One 8- to 10-ounce New York steak or any cut you prefer, trimmed of *all* fat
Salt
Freshly ground black pepper
4 cups loosely packed arugula leaves, trimmed, washed, and dried
1 tablespoon balsamic vinegar

1. Preheat a grill or broiler.

2. Combine 2 tablespoons olive oil with the garlic. Brush this mixture on the steak, coating well on both sides. Season with salt and pepper.

3. Cook steak to the desired doneness. When done, remove from the grill or broiler and let sit on a plate for 5 minutes, long enough for the meat to set and for it to be cool enough to handle. Slice the meat against the grain into ¼-inch-thick strips.

4. Toss the arugula with the remaining olive oil and the balsamic vinegar. Season with a pinch of salt and plenty of pepper. Add more oil or vinegar, if desired.

5. Lay the slices of steak on 2 plates. Pour the meat juices over the steak and cover with the arugula (the meat will barely be visible). Serve at once.

Smoked Ham, Belgian Endive, Watercress, and Hearts of Palm Salad

SERVES 4 AS A MAIN COURSE; 8 AS AN APPETIZER

One 4½-ounce can hearts of palm
4 Belgian endives (about 4 ounces each)
2 cups watercress leaves, large stems removed
½ cup julienned smoked ham (2 ounces), cut ⅛ inch by 2 inches
1 tablespoon freshly squeezed lemon juice
2 tablespoons champagne or other white wine vinegar
1 tablespoon Dijon mustard
½ cup peanut oil or other vegetable oil (not olive oil)
Salt
Freshly ground black pepper
1 tablespoon chopped chives

1. Drain the hearts of palm and cut them in half lengthwise. Remove the center if it is tough and woody. Cut the pieces into ½-inch lengths and place in a mixing bowl; you should have ½ cup.

2. Slice each endive in half lengthwise. Cut off the core at the base of each half, and slice the leaves into long strips, about 3 strips per leaf. Place in salad bowl.

3. Wash the watercress and spin dry. Make sure the larger bitter stems are removed. Add to the salad bowl.

4. Add the ham to the bowl.

5. Whisk together the lemon juice, vinegar, and mustard. Slowly add the oil and whisk until it is well incorporated. Season to taste with salt and pepper.

6. Add the vinaigrette to the salad and toss well. Add the chopped chives and toss again. Serve at once.

Pasta and Rice Salads

Starches benefit from the addition of strong flavors, such as cured meats, onions, powerful herbs, briny olives or capers, and certainly, garlic. These recipes are perfect for buffets and large parties because they can be made in advance and improve in flavor when refrigerated for a while before serving.

Arborio Rice Salad with Prosciutto and Peas

Bulgur Wheat Salad with Tomato, Onion, and Mint (Tabbouleh)

Italian Rice Salad with Shrimp, Fennel, and Basil

Orzo Salad with Feta, Olives, and Red Pepper

Warm Wild Rice Salad with Fall Mushrooms

Wild Rice Salad

Pasta Salad with Broiled Eggplant and Smoked Gouda

Pasta Salad with Grilled Vegetables

Pasta Salad Niçoise

Sicilian Pasta Salad

Pasta Shells with Seafood and Tapenade Vinaigrette

Arborio Rice Salad with Prosciutto and Peas

SERVES 6 TO 8

1 teaspoon minced garlic
1 tablespoon minced yellow onion
6 tablespoons freshly squeezed lemon juice
6 tablespoons red wine vinegar
2 tablespoons chopped Italian parsley
¾ cup extra-virgin olive oil
Salt
Freshly ground black pepper
1½ cups Italian arborio rice, cooked and chilled (page 204)
½ cup frozen peas
½ cup diced carrot (¼-inch dice)
½ cup julienned well-trimmed, thinly sliced prosciutto (2 ounces)

1. In a mixing bowl combine the garlic, onion, lemon juice, vinegar, parsley, and olive oil. Whisk well and season to taste with salt and pepper. Set aside.

2. Prepare an ice bath. Bring 2 cups water to a boil with ¼ teaspoon salt. Blanch the peas for 30 seconds and remove to the ice bath, using a slotted spoon. Blanch the diced carrot for 1 minute and remove to the ice bath. Drain the peas and carrots and add them to the vinaigrette. Add the prosciutto.

3. Remove the rice from the refrigerator and fold in the vinaigrette mixture. Mix well. Return to the refrigerator and chill for at least 2 hours before serving.

Bulgur Wheat Salad with Tomato, Onion, and Mint (Tabbouleh)

MAKES 6 CUPS

½ cup bulgur wheat
½ cup finely minced onion
½ teaspoon minced garlic
½ teaspoon ground allspice
1 teaspoon freshly ground black pepper
1½ teaspoons salt
½ cup freshly squeezed lemon juice
½ cup olive oil
3 cups finely chopped unpeeled seeded tomato (about 1¼ pounds)
2 cups finely chopped flat-leaf parsley
1 cup finely chopped scallions, equal amounts white and green
½ cup chopped spearmint
1 head butter, Bibb, or limestone lettuce leaves, washed and dried

1. Soak the bulgur in 3 cups cold water for 30 minutes. Scoop the wheat out of the water and squeeze it dry in your hands. Squeeze it, little by little, a second time to make sure it is as dry as possible. Place in a large mixing bowl and set aside.

2. In another bowl, combine the onion, garlic, allspice, pepper, salt, and lemon juice. Stir well to dissolve the salt. Whisk in the oil.

3. Add the tomato, parsley, scallions, and spearmint to the bulgur. Toss well with your hands, combining all the ingredients.

4. Add the dressing and stir very well. Check the seasoning. The tabbouleh may need more salt, pepper, lemon juice, or olive oil. Chill at least 2 hours before serving, and toss again just before serving. Surround a platter with lettuce leaves and use them to scoop up the salad.

Italian Rice Salad with Shrimp, Fennel, and Basil

SERVES 8

1½ cups arborio rice
Salt
8 tablespoons light olive oil
¾ pound large uncooked shrimp, with shells
Freshly ground black pepper
2 tablespoons dry white wine or dry vermouth
1 teaspoon minced garlic
½ teaspoon dried red pepper flakes
2 cups diced yellow onions
2 cups diced fennel bulb (two 6-ounce bulbs)
4 tablespoons red wine vinegar
4 tablespoons freshly squeezed lemon juice
3 tablespoons chopped fresh basil
2 cups diced unpeeled seeded tomatoes (2 large)

1. Wash the rice well with cold water while bringing 3 quarts water with 1½ teaspoons salt to a boil. Stir the rice into the water and simmer for 10 to 12 minutes, or until the rice is cooked through but not too soft. Immediately pour the rice into a colander or strainer and rinse with cold water to cool it completely and remove any excess starch. Dry the cooled rice well by spreading it on a towel. Once dry, place it in a large bowl and refrigerate.

2. Heat the light olive oil in a sauté pan. Pat the shrimp dry, season with a pinch of salt and pepper, and sauté until their shells turn red and the shrimp are almost cooked through, about 1½ minutes per side. Add the white wine or vermouth and continue cooking for 30 seconds more. Remove the shrimp and let them cool.

3. Add the garlic, dried red pepper flakes, pinch of black pepper, onions, and fennel to the olive oil and wine remaining in the pan. Stir well. Season with a pinch of salt and cook over medium heat until the fennel softens slightly and the onion becomes translucent. Do not brown. When done, remove this mixture and any liquid remaining in the sauté pan to a bowl and let cool.

4. Peel and devein the cooled shrimp, dice into ½-inch pieces, and add to the onion-fennel mixture.

5. In a small mixing bowl, whisk together the red wine vinegar, lemon juice, pinch of salt, extra-virgin olive oil, and the chopped basil.

6. Remove the cooled rice from the refrigerator and add the shrimp-onion-fennel mixture, the diced tomatoes, and the dressing. Mix well. Refrigerate for at least 2 hours before serving.

Orzo Salad with Feta, Olives and Red Pepper

SERVES 6 TO 8

Orzo is the Greek word for rice, though orzo is a pasta.

2 tablespoons olive oil
Salt
1 pound dry orzo
1 large red bell pepper
½ cup Greek olives, either Calamata or the dried oil-cured variety
  (about 2 ounces)
2 tablespoons chopped basil
¼ teaspoon minced garlic
1 tablespoon minced red or yellow onion
3 tablespoons freshly squeezed lemon juice
¼ teaspoon dried red pepper flakes
2 tablespoons red wine vinegar
6 tablespoons extra-virgin olive oil
Freshly ground black pepper
¼ pound feta cheese

1. Bring 4 quarts water to a boil. Add 1 tablespoon olive oil and 1 tablespoon salt. Add the orzo and cook until al dente, stirring occasionally (this pasta will cook in about 2 minutes because it is so small). Drain and toss with 1 tablespoon olive oil. Let cool.

2. Cut the bell pepper in half lengthwise. Remove the stem, seeds, and cartilage inside each half. Cut each half into ¼-inch strips; cut each strip into ¼-inch dice. This should yield about 1 cup diced pepper. Reserve.

3. Pit the olives and quarter them. Reserve.

4. Combine the basil, garlic, onion, lemon juice, red pepper flakes, and vinegar. Stir in the extra-virgin olive oil. Season with pepper and just a pinch of salt (there are salty ingredients in this dish).

5. In a mixing bowl, combine the pasta, diced peppers, and olives. Fold in the dressing and toss well. Refrigerate until ready to serve (up to 8 hours).

6. Before serving, slice and then crumble the feta over the salad. Toss and serve.

*W*arm Wild Rice Salad with Fall Mushrooms

SERVES 4 AS A MAIN COURSE

Make this in the fall or winter, when chanterelle and porcini mushrooms are available. Shiitake and oyster mushrooms, which are always available, make a more than adequate substitute at other times.

½ pound mushrooms, a combination of two or more mentioned above
3 tablespoons sherry or balsamic vinegar
6 tablespoons walnut oil or olive oil
Salt
Freshly ground black pepper
2 cups loosely packed white curly endive, washed and dried
¼ teaspoon minced garlic
2 cups cooked wild rice (see Wild Rice Salad, page 209)

1. Clean and trim the mushrooms; if you are using shiitakes, remove the stems (they are too tough) and save them (frozen, if

(continued)

you like) for a sauce or stock. The stems of the other three varieties are tender and should be used. Do not wet the mushrooms because they absorb too much water. If they have only a bit of dirt on them, wipe them clean with a damp cloth. If you must rinse them, dry them quickly and, using a clean cloth, gently squeeze as much water from them as possible.

2. Cut the mushrooms roughly into ¼-inch slices. Combine them in a bowl and set aside.

3. When ready to serve, whisk together 2 tablespoons vinegar with 2 tablespoons oil. Season to taste with salt and white pepper. Toss the curly endive with this vinegary dressing. Center the dressed greens on individual plates or on a serving platter.

4. Heat a large skillet until very hot. Add 4 tablespoons oil. Taking care not to splatter yourself, add the mushrooms. Sprinkle with salt and pepper and stir. After they have softened and released their moisture, continue cooking until they turn brown. Add the garlic, stir quickly, and add the remaining 1 tablespoon vinegar and the wild rice. Stir constantly, heating the rice.

5. Spoon the rice-mushroom mixture around the mound of endive and serve at once.

ild Rice Salad

SERVES 8

This salad resembles a wild rice Tabbouleh. It makes an excellent accompaniment to cold lamb or chicken.

4 cups cooked wild rice, cooled (see Note)
6 scallions, white parts only, minced
2 peeled, seeded, and diced tomatoes
2 tablespoons chopped mint leaves
2 tablespoons chopped parsley
4 tablespoons olive oil
4 tablespoons peanut oil or other vegetable oil
4 tablespoons freshly squeezed lemon juice
1½ teaspoons salt
1½ teaspoons freshly ground black pepper

1. Combine the cooled wild rice, scallions, tomatoes, mint, and parsley in a large bowl.

2. In a separate bowl, whisk together the oils, lemon juice, salt, and pepper. They will emulsify easily.

3. Pour dressing over the rice mixture and toss to combine. Let the salad stand in the refrigerator for at least 1 hour before serving.

NOTE To cook wild rice, wash 1 cup in cold water. Bring to a boil 1 quart water with ½ teaspoon salt added. Stir in the wild rice and return to a boil, stirring constantly. Reduce the heat and simmer, covered, for 50 minutes to 1 hour, or just until the kernels puff open. Uncover and fluff with a fork. Simmer for 5 minutes more. Drain and cool.

Pasta Salad with Broiled Eggplant and Smoked Gouda

SERVES 8

1 pound dry pasta (use a short shape such as penne)
Salt
8 tablespoons extra-virgin olive oil
1 tablespoon minced fresh oregano
1 teaspoon minced garlic
6 to 8 slices eggplant (½ inch thick; 1 medium eggplant)
Freshly ground black pepper
2 tablespoons minced red onion
2 tablespoons red wine vinegar
8 ounces smoked Gouda or smoked mozzarella, trimmed and cut into
   julienne strips ¼ inch by 1 inch
1 tablespoon coarsely chopped parsley

1. Preheat broiler. Bring 4 quarts water to a boil with 1 tablespoon salt and 1 tablespoon olive oil. Add the pasta and cook al dente, stirring occasionally. Drain and toss with 1 tablespoon olive oil. Lay on a baking sheet to cool.

2. Combine the remaining 6 tablespoons olive oil with the minced oregano and garlic.

3. Lay the eggplant on a baking sheet and lightly brush it on both sides with the olive oil–herb mixture. Do not use too much oil. Season with salt and pepper.

4. Broil the eggplant on both sides until soft and browned, but not mushy. Remove and cool to room temperature.

5. To the leftover olive oil—herb mixture, add the minced onion and red wine vinegar, along with a pinch of salt and pepper.

6. Cut the cooked eggplant into strips ½ inch by 1 inch. Place the pasta in a bowl and add the eggplant, Gouda or mozzarella, and chopped parsley.

7. Pour the dressing over the pasta and toss well. Serve at once or refrigerate. Remove from refrigerator 1 hour before serving.

$\mathscr{P}$asta Salad with Grilled Vegetables

SERVES 8

The subtle flavor of this salad comes entirely from the grilled vegetables. If you do not have a grill or barbecue available, wait until you do to make this dish.

1 pound dried pasta (use a short shape, such as fusilli)

Salt

1 tablespoon pure olive oil

7 tablespoons extra-virgin olive oil

3 tablespoons freshly squeezed lemon juice

2 tablespoons balsamic vinegar

¼ teaspoon minced garlic

1 teaspoon chopped fresh rosemary, or ½ teaspoon dried

2 teaspoons chopped fresh oregano, or 1 teaspoon dried

2 teaspoons chopped fresh basil, or 1 teaspoon dried

½ teaspoon freshly ground black pepper

8 ounces eggplant (about 2 cups), peeled and sliced into ⅜-inch pieces (use about half of a large eggplant weighing about 1¼ pounds, or use 2 small Japanese eggplants)

1 medium zucchini, skin on, the ends trimmed, sliced lengthwise into ¼-inch pieces

1 medium yellow crookneck squash, prepared like the zucchini

1 medium Bermuda onion, peeled and cut into ½-inch slices

1 small carrot, peeled, trimmed, and cut into ¼-inch slices

1 small head of radicchio (about 4 inches in diameter, weighing about 5 ounces); cut lengthwise into quarters with base still attached

1 head Belgian endive (3 to 4 ounces), halved lengthwise

One 8-ounce fennel bulb, stems and leaves removed, sliced lengthwise into ¼-inch pieces

Two 2-inch shiitake mushrooms, stems removed

1. Preheat the grill.

2. Cook the pasta in boiling water with 1 tablespoon each salt and oil, stirring occasionally, until al dente. Drain and toss with 1 tablespoon extra-virgin olive oil. Spread the pasta on a cookie sheet and allow it to cool.

3. In a small mixing bowl, combine the extra-virgin olive oil, lemon juice, balsamic vinegar, garlic, herbs, ½ teaspoon salt, and the pepper.

4. On a baking sheet or large platter, lay out all of the vegetables. Brush the vegetables with the herb dressing, stirring the dressing often.

5. Grill the vegetables on both sides until cooked, but not mushy. These taste best slightly charred but still crunchy. As the vegetables are cooked, remove them to another baking sheet, spreading them out to cool.

6. Once cooled, cut the vegetables into ½-inch pieces.

7. Put the cooled pasta into a large mixing bowl. Add the grilled vegetables and toss well. Add the remaining herb dressing and toss again.

8. Serve at room temperature, or refrigerate for future serving.

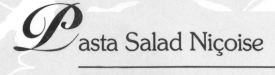asta Salad Niçoise

SERVES 6 TO 8

3 tablespoons pure olive oil

Salt

1 pound pasta, preferably small shapes such as fusilli, orrecchiete, or farfalle

¼ cup chopped carrot

¼ cup chopped celery

½ cup green beans, trimmed and cut into 1-inch pieces

½ cup scallions, cut into 1-inch pieces (equal amounts white and green)

6 tablespoons extra-virgin olive oil

2 tablespoons freshly squeezed lemon juice

¼ teaspoon minced garlic

Freshly ground black pepper

One 6½-ounce can Italian-style tuna packed in olive oil

3 radishes, thinly sliced

½ cup diced unpeeled seeded tomato

½ cup pitted black olives, preferably Niçoise or Calamata

¼ cup drained capers

2 tablespoons coarsely chopped Italian parsley

1. Add 1 tablespoon each pure olive oil and salt to 4 quarts boiling water. Add the pasta and cook until al dente. Drain, toss with 1 more tablespoon oil, and let cool.

2. Add 1 tablespoon salt to 2 quarts boiling water. Have an ice bath ready. Quickly blanch the diced carrot, celery, green beans, and scallions in the boiling water for 1 minute. Drain and submerge immediately in the ice bath to stop the cooking and preserve the bright colors.

3. Make a dressing by whisking together the extra-virgin olive oil, lemon juice, and garlic. Season with ¼ teaspoon salt and a generous amount of freshly ground black pepper

4. Assemble the pasta salad by tossing together all of the ingredients and adding the dressing. Let it stand in the refrigerator for at least 1 hour to allow the flavors to combine. Bring to room temperature before serving.

Sicilian Pasta Salad

SERVES 8

Salt

1 tablespoon pure olive oil

1 pound dried pasta (use a short shape, such as penne or rigatoni)

9 tablespoons extra-virgin olive oil

¼ cup cubed zucchini (¼-inch cubes)

2 ounces Genoa salami, sliced ⅛-inch thick and julienned (½ cup)

2 ounces mortadella, sliced ⅛-inch thick and julienned (½ cup)

2 ounces capocollo, fat removed, sliced ⅛-inch thick and julienned (½ cup)

2 ounces provolone, cut into ¼-inch cubes (½ cup)

2 ounces fresh mozzarella, cut into ¼-inch cubes (½ cup)

½ cup diced unpeeled seeded tomato (1 medium)

½ cup diced red bell pepper

¼ cup chopped green olives

¼ cup pepperoncini (hot Italian peppers), stems and seeds removed, julienned

2 tablespoons red wine vinegar

2 tablespoons freshly squeezed lemon juice

1 tablespoon chopped fresh oregano

2 tablespoons chopped fresh basil

1 tablespoon minced yellow onion

1 teaspoon minced garlic

¼ teaspoon freshly ground black pepper

¼ teaspoon dried red pepper flakes

1. Bring 4 quarts water to a boil with 1 tablespoon salt and 1 tablespoon pure olive oil. Add the pasta and cook until al dente, stirring occasionally. Drain and toss with 1 tablespoon extra-virgin olive oil. Cool.

2. Prepare an ice bath. Bring 2 cups water to a boil with ¼ teaspoon salt. Add the diced zucchini and blanch for 1 minute. Drain the zucchini and plunge it immediately into the ice water to stop the cooking and preserve the color. Drain.

3. Place the cooled pasta in a large mixing bowl. Add the salami, mortadella, capocollo, provolone, mozzarella, zucchini, tomato, bell pepper, olives, and pepperoncini.

4. In a small mixing bowl, mix together the red wine vinegar, lemon juice, oregano, basil, onion, garlic, black pepper, red pepper flakes, and ¼ teaspoon salt. Slowly whisk in the remaining olive oil.

5. Add this dressing to the other ingredients and toss well. If possible, allow the pasta to sit for 1 or 2 hours, covered, in the refrigerator. Serve chilled.

Pasta Shells with Seafood and Tapenade Vinaigrette

SERVES 4

The aroma of the cooking liquid from the mussels and clams enhances the already intense flavors of the tapenade.

½ pound dry pasta (shells or another short variety)
Salt
Approximately ½ cup extra-virgin olive oil
½ pound mussels
½ pound clams
2 teaspoons minced shallots or yellow onion
2 teaspoons minced garlic
1 cup dry white wine
½ pound bay scallops
Freshly ground white pepper
½ pound medium shrimp, cooked, shelled, and deveined (see Cooked Shrimp for Salads, page 256)
⅓ cup Tapenade (page 243)
1 tablespoon freshly squeezed lemon juice
⅛ teaspoon dried red pepper flakes
1 tablespoon coarsely chopped parsley

1. Bring 2 quarts water to a boil with 1½ teaspoons salt and 1 tablespoon olive oil. Cook the pasta until al dente, stirring occasionally as it cooks. Drain and toss with 1 tablespoon olive oil. Cool on a platter or baking sheet.

2. Cook the mussels and clams with the shallots, garlic, and wine, following steps 1 through 3 on pages 116–17, Seafood Salad with Saffron and Root Vegetables.

3. Strain the liquid that has collected in the bowl under the colander. Place it in a saucepan and reduce it by half.

4. While the liquid is reducing, cook the scallops. Heat a sauté pan very hot. Add 1 tablespoon olive oil. Pat the scallops dry and season with salt and pepper. Place in pan and brown them quickly; they should still be soft in the center. Remove to a bowl and let cool to room temperature.

5. Cut the cooked shrimp into small pieces roughly the size of bay scallops. Add to the chilling mussels and clams.

6. When the mussel-clam cooking liquid is sufficiently reduced, remove to a bowl and chill.

7. In a large mixing bowl, combine all of the chilled cooked seafood: the mussels, clams, shrimp, and bay scallops. Coat with 2 tablespoons reduced cooking liquid and toss.

8. In a small bowl, combine another 4 tablespoons reduced cooking liquid with the tapenade and whisk well. Add 1 tablespoon olive oil, the lemon juice, and the red pepper flakes. Whisk again.

9. Add the pasta to the seafood. Toss with the tapenade vinaigrette. Sprinkle with parsley and serve on a platter or in a bowl, or refrigerate for up to 24 hours before serving.

Legumes

Like pastas and rice, legumes benefit from the aggressive flavors of citrus juices and vinegars. Healthy and satisfying, bean salads are increasing in popularity.

Five-Bean Salad

Lentil Salad with Bacon and Walnuts

Marinated Chick-Peas (Garbanzo Bean Salad)

Mediterranean Three-Bean Salad with Cumin Vinaigrette

Cannelini Beans with Mint and Cured Meats

Spicy Black Bean Salad with Cilantro and Tomato

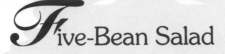

Five-Bean Salad

MAKES 3 PINTS; 8 SERVINGS

¼ cup dried white beans, such as cannelini or Great Northern
¼ cup dried pink or red beans
¼ cup dried navy or kidney beans
Salt
¼ pound yellow wax beans
¼ pound green beans, such as Kentucky or haricots verts
2 cups white vinegar, preferably imported champagne or tarragon
  vinegar
½ cup sugar
1 teaspoon chopped fresh tarragon, or 1 teaspoon dried
2 cloves garlic, peeled and slightly smashed
1 teaspoon pickling spice
¼ cup diced yellow onion
Freshly ground white pepper

1. Soak the dried beans overnight in 6 cups of water. The next day, add 2 cups water and ½ teaspoon salt and bring to a boil. Reduce heat and simmer for 25 to 30 minutes, or until tender but not mushy. Drain the cooked beans and place in a large mixing bowl.

2. Prepare a large ice bath. Trim both varieties of fresh beans. Cook them in 2 quarts boiling water to which 1 teaspoon salt has been added; cook for 1 to 2 minutes, or until the beans are cooked but still crunchy. Remove from the boiling water and plunge immediately into the ice bath to stop the cooking and preserve the color. Drain and add to the mixing bowl.

3. Bring the vinegar, ½ cup water, and sugar to a boil and simmer for 1 minute.

4. Wrap the tarragon, garlic, and pickling spice in cheesecloth and tie well with kitchen twine.

5. Place this cheesecloth ball in a small mixing bowl along with the chopped onion. Pour the vinegar mixture over the cheesecloth ball and onion. Let cool until lukewarm.

6. Pour the liquid mixture over the cooked beans and mix well. Adjust the seasoning with salt and pepper. Refrigerate overnight. Remove the cheesecloth ball before serving.

Lentil Salad with Bacon and Walnuts

MAKES ABOUT 2 CUPS; 4 SERVINGS

Serve this as a side dish with grilled meats or fowl, or spoon it over limestone lettuce that has also been seasoned with walnut oil and sherry vinegar, for an interesting mixed green salad.

¼ cup dried lentils (preferably French Lentilles de Puy)
Salt
2 thin slices smoked bacon
1 tablespoon minced onion
3 tablespoons walnut oil
1 tablespoon sherry vinegar
¼ cup finely chopped, peeled, seeded tomato
¼ cup chopped freshly shelled walnuts
Freshly ground black pepper

1. Rinse the lentils in a colander or strainer.

2. Bring the lentils to a boil in 1 quart water to which ½ teaspoon salt has been added. Reduce heat and simmer for approximately 20 minutes, until they are tender but not mushy. It is important that the lentils not break up. When they are done, drain and rinse with cold water to stop cooking.

3. While the lentils are cooking, fry the bacon until crisp. Remove from the pan and drain on a paper towel. Chop the bacon into pieces approximately ¼-inch square and reserve.

4. In the bacon fat, cook the onion until it is half-cooked, soft but not translucent. Remove from the pan with a strainer or a slotted spoon. Discard all but 1 teaspoon fat.

5. Combine the remaining bacon fat with the walnut oil, sherry vinegar, onion, and minced bacon. Season to taste with pepper.

6. In a mixing bowl, combine the cooked lentils with the tomato, walnuts, and dressing. Toss well. Take care not to break the lentils. Check the seasoning and add salt or pepper, if desired. Serve at once or chill and serve later. This salad keeps for 2 days in the refrigerator.

$\mathscr{M}$arinated Chick-Peas (Garbanzo Bean Salad)

MAKES ABOUT 3 CUPS; 4 SERVINGS

¾ cup dried chick-peas
1½ teaspoons salt
½ cup finely chopped fennel or celery
¼ cup finely chopped red onion
½ teaspoon minced garlic
1 teaspoon chopped fresh oregano, or ½ teaspoon dried
½ cup olive oil
¼ cup freshly squeezed lemon juice
1 small tomato, peeled, seeded, and finely chopped (about ½ cup)
½ teaspoon freshly ground black pepper

1. Rinse the chick-peas under cold running water in a strainer. Pick out any stones or foreign matter. Soak them in 3 cups water overnight in the refrigerator. Discard any that float to the surface.

2. Place the chick-peas and their soaking liquid in a saucepan, add 1 teaspoon salt and stir. Bring to a boil, reduce heat to a simmer, and cook, partially covered, for 35 to 45 minutes, or until they are tender but not mushy. Skim any foam that rises to the surface during cooking. Remove from the heat and let cool slightly in the liquid.

3. When the chick-peas are still warm, strain them, reserving ¼ cup liquid. Place them in a large bowl. Add the fennel and onion and toss well.

4. In a small mixing bowl, combine the minced garlic, oregano, olive oil, lemon juice, reserved cooking liquid, chopped tomato, the remaining ½ teaspoon salt and the pepper. Stir together well and pour over the chick-peas. Mix well with a large spoon. Refrigerate 2 hours before serving.

Mediterranean Three-Bean Salad with Cumin Vinaigrette

MAKES 2 PINTS

1 cup dried lentils
1 cup dried cannelini or baby lima beans
1 cup dried chick-peas (garbanzos)
Salt
1 cup chopped Bermuda onion or any other sweet onion
1 cup seeded chopped tomato
¾ coarsely chopped pitted Calamata olives
1 teaspoon ground cumin
⅛ teaspoon ground cinnamon
⅛ teaspoon paprika
1 teaspoon sugar
4 tablespoons freshly squeezed lemon juice
1 tablespoon Dijon mustard
1 teaspoon minced garlic
½ cup extra-virgin olive oil
3 tablespoons chopped cilantro
Freshly ground black pepper

1. Soak each variety of dried beans separately in 2 cups of water, overnight.

2. Add 2 cups water and a ½ teaspoon salt to each of the three types of beans and bring to a boil. Simmer for 20 to 30 minutes, depending on the bean, or until cooked but not mushy. Drain and combine the beans in a mixing bowl.

3. Add the onion, tomato, and olives to the bowl. Toss gently.

4. Prepare the vinaigrette by whisking together the remaining ingredients, except the pepper.

(continued)

5. While the beans are still warm, add the vinaigrette and toss gently. Season to taste with salt and pepper. Chill for at least 2 hours before serving.

Cannelini Beans with Mint and Cured Meats

SERVES 4 AS A FIRST COURSE

The subtle freshness of mint is an excellent foil for the saltiness of the cured meats in this simple salad.

2 cups Cooked Cannelini Beans (page 254)
2 tablespoons chopped fresh spearmint, or 1 tablespoon chopped fresh peppermint (see Note)
½ pound thinly sliced assorted cured meats, such as imported Italian prosciutto di Parma, salami, mortadella, coppa secco, etc.
1 tablespoon extra-virgin olive oil
Freshly ground black pepper

1. Mix the beans gently with the chopped mint, taking care to break as few beans as possible. Lay the beans in a thin layer on a large platter.

2. Cover the beans with the cured meats, overlapping the varieties slightly.

3. Drizzle with the olive oil. Season with a few grinds of pepper and serve at once.

NOTE Your grocer may not specify which mint is available. Spearmint has rough, light green leaves, which are somewhat flimsy, whereas peppermint has a stiffer, smooth, dark, shiny leaf.

Spicy Black Bean Salad with Cilantro and Tomato

MAKES 3 CUPS

1 cup dried black beans
1½ teaspoons salt
¼ cup finely chopped red onion
1 small seeded jalapeño or serrano chili, finely minced (see Note)
¼ cup finely chopped celery
1 cup finely chopped peeled seeded tomato
½ cup olive oil
¼ cup freshly squeezed lime juice
⅓ cup coarsely chopped cilantro

1. Rinse the beans well under cold running water. Pick out any pebbles or other foreign matter. Soak in 3 cups water overnight, refrigerated.

2. Bring the beans and 1 teaspoon salt to a boil in the soaking water. Reduce heat to a simmer and cook, partially covered, until tender and not grainy, about 1 hour. Let the beans cool in their liquid.

3. While still slightly warm, strain the beans and discard the liquid. Place the beans in a large bowl. Add the onion, chili, and celery. Set aside.

4. In a small bowl, combine the tomato, oil, lime juice, cilantro, and the remaining ½ teaspoon salt. Stir well. Pour mixture over the beans and toss well. Chill for 2 hours before serving.

NOTE The amount of chili can be reduced according to taste. It can, in fact, be omitted entirely. In that case, add some pepper to the vinaigrette.

Fruit

The less done with fruit to change its nature, the more enjoyable it is to eat. Here are a few recipes that offer differing points of view on how best to leave well enough alone.

$\mathcal{A}$pple, Celery, and Walnut Salad with Grapes

MAKES ABOUT 3½ CUPS; 4 SERVINGS

This Waldorf salad is delicious.

1 cup diced, cored, and peeled Granny Smith or Pippin apple
   (½-inch dice)
1 tablespoon freshly squeezed lemon juice
1 diced celery (½-inch dice)
1 cup seedless grapes, preferably Red Flame, halved
½ cup coarsely chopped walnuts
1 teaspoon Dijon mustard
¾ to 1 cup mayonnaise

1. In a bowl, combine the apple, lemon juice, celery, grapes, and walnuts. Mix well.

2. In a separate bowl, whisk together the mustard and mayonnaise.

3. Fold the seasoned mayonnaise into the salad and toss well. Chill before serving.

Chopped Fruit with Lime and Mint

MAKES 1 QUART; 4 TO 6 SERVINGS

The list of fruit and the quantities given are just guidelines. This is a casual recipe that lends itself well to substitutions and personal preferences.

2 tablespoons freshly squeezed lime juice
1 large orange, preferably navel
1 grapefruit, preferably pink
1 tart green apple
1 cup diced melon (cantaloupe, honeydew, or casaba)
1 cup diced pineapple
½ cup red or green seedless grapes, halved
1 banana, peeled and sliced
6 strawberries, washed, hulled, and quartered
A few mint leaves for garnish

1. Put the lime juice in a bowl large enough to accommodate the finished salad. With a paring knife, remove the skin and all of the white membranes from the orange and grapefruit. Cut out the segments and remove the seeds. Cut each segment into 2 or 3 pieces. Work directly over the bowl to capture any juices that fall from the fruit while cutting them. Add the cut orange and grapefruit segments to the bowl.

2. Peel the apple and dice it into pieces about the same size as the citrus segments. Add to the mixing bowl immediately and mix well. The acidity of the citrus juices will prevent the apple from discoloring.

3. Add the remaining fruit to the bowl.

4. Add the chopped mint and toss well. If possible, refrigerate for 1 hour before serving. Garnish with mint leaves before serving.

*C*itrus Salad with Bermuda Onion and Balsamic Vinegar

A wonderful chef and cookbook writer friend of mine, Evan Klei-man, once served me grilled fresh sardines with orange segments, onion, and a drop of olive oil. That garnish is the inspiration for this salad.

1 small Bermuda onion
1 tablespoon balsamic vinegar
1 pink grapefruit
2 blood oranges
2 tangerines
Salt
Freshly ground black pepper
2 tablespoons extra-virgin olive oil

1. Peel the onion. Slice it into paper-thin rings, enough to make ½ cup.

2. Lay the onion slices in a bowl. Add the balsamic vinegar and toss. Reserve.

3. Peel all the fruit, removing all the skin and the white pith. Squeeze the juice contained in the skin into a bowl to collect 4 tablespoons. Reserve.

4. Slice all the fruit into circles. If the rounds of grapefruit and orange are large and unwieldy, cut them in half or thirds. Discard any pits and save any juices that collect on the cutting board. Add these to the other juices.

5. Lay the rounds of fruit on a platter, alternating pieces of fruit and slices of marinated onion. Pour any vinegar remaining in the bowl over the fruit and onion on the platter.

6. In a small mixing bowl, combine the fruit juice with a pinch of salt and pepper. Whisk in the olive oil. Pour mixture over fruit and onion and serve at once, or cover the platter and refrigerate for several hours before serving.

Mango, Pineapple, and Grapefruit Salad with Poppy Seed–Yogurt Dressing

1 cup cubed mango (½-inch cubes) (see Note)

1 cup grapefruit segments, preferably pink, all white skin and membranes removed

1 cup ½-inch pineapple cubes

4 tablespoons collected juice from cutting the grapefruit and pineapple (if you don't have enough, supplement with orange, lemon, or lime juice)

½ cup plain yogurt (regular, low-fat, or nonfat)

2 tablespoons honey

1½ teaspoons poppy seeds

1. Very gently mix together the mango, grapefruit, and pineapple in a bowl. Take care not to crush the pieces.

2. Whisk together the juice, yogurt, 1 tablespoon honey, and half the poppy seeds.

3. Spread the sauce onto plates. Leave some plate visible around the border.

4. Evenly distribute the fruit mixture on top of the yogurt. Drizzle the remaining 1 tablespoon over the fruit and yogurt. Sprinkle with the remaining poppy seeds and serve at once.

NOTE To cut the mango, place the fruit on a cutting board. Using a thin, sharp knife, cut off the top third horizontally, cutting around the large, flat seed. Turn the mango over and repeat. If the flesh on the outer edges of the seed is not too fibrous, cut it away and slice it thinly. Otherwise, do not use it for this salad. Cut each of the thirds in half lengthwise and remove their skin, much the way you would the rind of a lemon. Cut into ½-inch cubes.

Strawberry and Melon Salad with Banana-Yogurt Dressing

You can combine this dressing with many fruits.

½ cup plain yogurt (regular, low-fat, or nonfat)
1 ripe banana
½ cup orange juice
2 ripe melons (use 2 of the following varieties: cantaloupe, honeydew, casaba, musk, or crenshaw)
1 pint strawberries

1. In a blender or food processor, purée the yogurt, banana, and orange juice. Reserve chilled.

2. Peel and cube the melons. Reserve.

3. Rinse the strawberries, then remove stems (in that order, so as not to get water inside the berries). Quarter them lengthwise.

4. Mix the melon with the dressing. Place in a serving bowl. Garnish with the strawberries and serve at once.

Vinaigrettes, Dressings, Sauces, and Condiments

Chinese Barbecue Sauce

MAKES 2½ CUPS

One 7-ounce jar plum sauce
3 tablespoons rice-wine vinegar
1½ teaspoons drained prepared horseradish
1½ teaspoons chili oil
½ teaspoon paprika
Pinch of ground cinnamon
Pinch of Chinese 5-spice powder
1 tablespoon Oriental sesame oil
One 7-ounce jar hoisin sauce
1½ cups duck or chicken stock, or canned low-salt chicken broth.
2 tablespoons freshly squeezed lime juice

1. In a heavy 2- or 3-quart saucepan over medium-high heat, bring the plum sauce to a boil. Reduce it by two-thirds, until it begins to caramelize.

2. Whisk in the rice-wine vinegar.

3. Add the horseradish, chili oil, paprika, cinnamon, and 5-spice powder; boil for 1 minute, whisking constantly.

4. Add the sesame oil and the hoisin sauce. Return to a boil and allow mixture to reduce slightly.

5. Add the stock. Return back to a boil and cook for 5 minutes, whisking occasionally.

6. Stir in the lime juice, return to a boil, and remove sauce from heat.

7. Use immediately or cool and store in the refrigerator.

$\mathcal{R}$ed Wine Sauce or Bordelaise

4 large shallots, finely minced
1 bay leaf
3 sprigs fresh thyme
¼ teaspoon crushed peppercorns
¼ teaspoon minced garlic
4 tablespoons unsalted butter, softened
1 bottle strong red wine, such as Cabernet, Burgundy, or Bordeaux
4 cups veal or chicken stock or canned low-salt chicken broth
Salt

1. In a heavy saucepan over medium heat, sweat the shallots, bay leaf, thyme, pepper, and garlic in 1 tablespoon butter until soft.

2. Add the wine and reduce over high heat until almost dry.

3. Add the stock and reduce by half.

4. Strain through a fine-mesh strainer.

5. Slowly whisk in the remaining butter. Salt to taste.

Rémoulade Sauce

½ cup mayonnaise
¼ cup finely minced celery
2 tablespoons finely minced scallion (equal amounts of white and green parts)
2 tablespoons chopped Italian parsley
1 tablespoon finely minced drained capers
1 tablespoon finely minced drained cornichons
1½ teaspoons freshly squeezed lemon juice
1½ teaspoons champagne vinegar
1 tablespoon liquid from jar of capers
1 tablespoon liquid from jar of cornichons
Salt
Freshly ground white pepper

Whisk the mayonnaise to loosen its consistency. Stir in the remaining ingredients. Mix well. Refrigerate until needed.

Tapenade (Olive, Anchovy, and Caper Purée)

MAKES 1 CUP

This Provençal purée can be used as a condiment, spread on bread or meat; it can also be thinned with more olive oil and some vinegar to become a vinaigrette or dip.

1 cup whole Calamata olives or another strong, black, Mediterranean variety
4 anchovy fillets, rinsed under cold water and patted dry
1 tablespoon minced garlic
2 tablespoons capers, drained and rinsed under cold water
3 tablespoons finely chopped fresh basil
2 tablespoons freshly squeezed lemon juice
⅓ cup extra-virgin olive oil
Freshly ground black pepper

1. Remove and discard the pits from the olives. Finely chop the olive meat. This should yield about ½ cup, packed. Finely chop the anchovies as well.

2. In a food processor or blender, combine the chopped olives, anchovies, garlic, capers, basil, and lemon juice. Blend to form a coarse purée.

3. In a thin stream, add half the olive oil. Check the consistency, which should be that of a thin, spreadable paste. Add more oil as needed. Season to taste with pepper.

4. Remove to a bowl, cover, and chill, preferably for several hours, before using.

Cilantro Vinaigrette

MAKES 2 CUPS

1 tablespoon grated peeled fresh ginger
¾ cup finely sliced scallions (white part and 1 inch of green)
½ cup rice-wine vinegar
1 teaspoon wasabi powder
¼ teaspoon salt
¼ teaspoon Chinese 5-spice powder
¼ cup cilantro leaves
1 cup peanut oil

1. In a blender or food processor, purée the ginger and scallions with the rice-wine vinegar, wasabi, salt, and 5-spice powder.

2. Add the cilantro and, with the blender or processor running, slowly add the oil in a thin stream. Once all the oil has been added, blend for an additional 15 seconds.

3. Use immediately or store in the refrigerator.

Japanese Vinaigrette

MAKES 2 CUPS

This recipe works very well as a marinade for shrimp, chicken, and fish, especially tuna, bass, scallops, and mahimahi. It is also a good accompaniment to salads with daikon, daikon sprouts, cucumber, carrot, celery, and watercress. Finally, it makes a delicious dipping sauce for tuna, halibut, or yellowtail sashimi.

1 cup peanut oil
4 tablespoons soy sauce
3 tablespoons Oriental sesame oil
3 tablespoons rice-wine vinegar
1 tablespoon freshly squeezed lemon juice
1 tablespoon freshly squeezed lime juice
3 tablespoons minced peeled fresh ginger (start with 3 walnut-size pieces)
3 tablespoons packed dark brown sugar
½ teaspoon minced garlic
2 teaspoons minced onion
2 teaspoons minced shallots
1 teaspoon drained prepared horseradish or freshly grated horseradish
½ teaspoon wasabi powder

1. Whisk together all the liquid ingredients.

2. Place the remaining ingredients in the bowl of a food processor fitted with the steel knife, or a blender jar, and add half the liquid ingredients. Process or blend well.

3. Whisk this sauce into the other half of the liquid ingredients, then strain the sauce through a fine sieve.

4. Store refrigerated.

Creamy Blue Cheese Dressing

MAKES 2 CUPS

This recipe can be cut in half to make 1 cup, but it hardly seems worth it. One uses more of this dressing per salad than one would use of an oil-based dressing. Furthermore, the dressing keeps well for a week if it is refrigerated.

1 tablespoon red wine vinegar
½ cup sour cream
½ cup mayonnaise
4 tablespoons buttermilk
¼ teaspoon minced garlic
½ teaspoon Worcestershire sauce
⅛ teaspoon Tabasco
½ teaspoon ground black pepper
¼ pound crumbled blue or Roquefort cheese

1. Thoroughly whisk together all of the ingredients *except* the cheese.

2. When well blended, stir in the crumbled cheese.

Creamy Herb Dressing

MAKES ABOUT 1 CUP

½ cup mayonnaise

2 teaspoons Dijon mustard

2 teaspoons chopped fresh herbs, such as tarragon, basil, dill,
    or chives, or a combination

4 tablespoons red wine, champagne, or tarragon vinegar

⅛ teaspoon salt

¼ teaspoon freshly ground white pepper

In a mixing bowl, whisk together the mayonnaise, mustard, chopped herbs, vinegar, salt, and pepper. The dressing should be thick, yet pourable. If it is too thick, add a few drops of water.

VARIATIONS

1. Substitute lemon juice for the vinegar.

2. Make a creamy garlic dressing by substituting finely minced garlic for the herbs and freshly ground black pepper for the white pepper.

*T*arragon Cream Dressing

MAKES ABOUT ½ CUP

This dressing is best made in the summer when fresh tarragon is plentiful and inexpensive. It has a bright flavor that is pleasant company for cooked, chilled vegetables and leftover cooked meats.

1½ teaspoons Dijon mustard
1 tablespoon coarse-grained mustard
1 tablespoon chopped fresh tarragon leaves, or 1½ teaspoons dried
2 tablespoons sherry vinegar
4 tablespoons olive oil or walnut oil
2 tablespoons heavy cream
Salt
Freshly ground white pepper

1. Whisk together the two mustards, chopped tarragon, and vinegar.

2. Slowly add the oil, drop by drop at first, allowing it to be incorporated.

3. Whisk in the cream.

4. Season to taste with salt and a generous amount of pepper.

5. Allow to sit in the refrigerator for at least 1 hour before using.

Thousand Island Dressing

MAKES 1½ CUPS

1 teaspoon sugar
1 teaspoon wine vinegar
1 teaspoon Worcestershire sauce
⅓ cup ketchup
⅔ cup mayonnaise
2 tablespoons minced scallion (white part only)
2 tablespoons minced red bell pepper (¼ small pepper)
3 tablespoons minced pickle (sweet or dill bread-and-butter variety)
1 tablespoon chopped parsley
1 hard-boiled egg
Freshly ground white pepper

1. In a small mixing bowl, dissolve the sugar in the vinegar. Add the Worcestershire and ketchup. Whisk well.

2. Whisk in the mayonnaise

3. Stir in the scallion, bell pepper, pickle, and parsley.

4. Separate the hard-boiled egg. Sieve the yolk into the sauce. Chop the white and add it as well. Stir well. Check the seasoning and add more pepper, if necessary. Keep refrigerated.

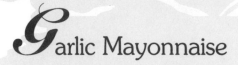

Garlic Mayonnaise

MAKES 1 CUP

This sauce is related to aïoli, a garlic mayonnaise from the south of France. There, the mayonnaise is made entirely from extra-virgin olive oil and is much heavier and less digestible. This recipe adds a small quantity of rich oil to a "regular" mayonnaise, making it more palatable to our taste. Use this sauce as a garnish for raw or cooked vegetables, grilled fish, or roasted meats.

1 tablespoon very finely minced garlic (preferably mashed to a paste
    with a mortar and pestle)
1 cup mayonnaise
3 to 4 tablespoons extra-virgin olive oil
1 tablespoon lemon juice
⅛ teaspoon ground cayenne

1. Whisk the garlic into the mayonnaise.

2. Whisk in the olive oil, lemon juice, and cayenne. Refrigerate until needed.

Garlic-Herb Marinade for Grilling

MAKES ABOUT 1¼ CUPS

You will find this to be a highly seasoned oil—great for brushing on vegetables, fish, poultry, or pork right before grilling or broiling.

1 cup extra-virgin olive oil
1 tablespoon finely minced fresh rosemary leaves
1 tablespoon finely minced fresh oregano leaves
1 tablespoon finely minced fresh thyme leaves
Peeled cloves from an entire 1½-ounce head of garlic, approximately
    12 cloves, left whole

Combine all ingredients and let sit at room temperature for at least 3 hours before using.

NOTE If fresh herbs are not available, dried can be substituted, although I do not encourage it. Use half the amount of each herb if you use dried. Also, the proportion of one herb to another can be adjusted to suit your own taste.

Basic Preparations

Cooked Cannelini Beans

1 cup dried cannelini beans
2 sprigs fresh thyme or rosemary or a combination (¼ teaspoon dried thyme and ⅛ teaspoon dried rosemary may be substituted)
4 parsley stems
1 clove garlic, unpeeled
1 bay leaf
1 stalk celery, cut in half
1 medium carrot, peeled and cut in half
1 small onion, peeled and cut in half
1 teaspoon salt
1 tablespoon olive oil
1 teaspoon freshly squeezed lemon juice
⅛ teaspoon minced garlic

1. Wash the beans under cold water. Soak them overnight in 4 cups water. After soaking, a few may float to the surface. Discard them. (If you forget to soak the beans overnight, cover them with 4 cups of water, bring to a boil, simmer for 2 minutes, and remove from the heat. Cover the pan and let sit for 1 hour. Proceed with the recipe.)

2. Make bouquet garni by tying together the fresh thyme and/ or rosemary, parsley stems, garlic, bay leaf, and celery. If using dried herbs, do not include them in the bouquet garni.

3. Place the beans in a pot, along with the water in which they soaked, the bouquet garni, and the dried thyme and/or rosemary, if using. Add the carrot, onion, and salt; stir well. Bring the pot to a boil, then reduce heat and simmer for about 1 hour, or until the beans are tender but not mushy. Remove from the heat and drain. Discard the bouquet garni, carrot, and onion.

4. Mix together the olive oil, lemon juice, and garlic. While the beans are still warm, gently add this mixture to them. They will readily absorb the dressing, which will enhance their flavor when chilled.

Cooked Shrimp for Salads

---

4 quarts Court Bouillon (next page), at room temperature
2 pounds shrimp, preferably in their shells (see Note)

1. Prepare an ice bath.

2. In a large pot combine the court bouillon and the shrimp. Bring to just below the boiling point (do not allow the pot to come to a full boil), reduce heat, and simmer for approximately 5 minutes, or until the shrimp just begin to curl. Drain the liquid.

3. Submerge the shrimp in ice water to stop cooking. Drain.

4. Peel and devein the shrimp.

5. Keep chilled until ready to serve.

NOTE The shrimp will be more flavorful when cooked with the shells on.

Court Bouillon

MAKES 4 QUARTS

3 quarts water
1 bottle (750 ml) dry white wine
1 cup white wine vinegar
1 teaspoon dried thyme
2 bay leaves
12 whole black or white peppercorns
2 onions, peeled and coarsely chopped
2 stalks celery with leaves, coarsely chopped
2 medium carrots, peeled and coarsely chopped
4 sprigs parsley
1 tablespoon salt

1. Bring all of the ingredients to a boil in a large pot. Simmer for 30 minutes. Strain, keeping the liquid and discarding the other ingredients.

2. Let the liquid cool to room temperature before using.

3. The court bouillon will keep up to a week in the refrigerator. It can also be frozen.

$\mathcal{H}$ow to Bone a Duck
(or Other Large Poultry)

1. It must be said that the difference between this being a difficult or an easy task is the sharpness of the knife you are using. *Use a sharp poultry boning knife!*

2. Inside the cavity of the duck, you may find a package containing the liver, gizzard, and neck. Remove it. Save the neck and gizzard, along with the carcass, for stock. The liver should not be used in stock because of its high content of blood. It can be frozen until you have saved enough duck and chicken livers to make a mousse or salad with them.

3. Remove the first 2 sections of the wing at the joint where they are connected to the small drummette attached to the breast. The removed sections should be saved with the carcass for stock.

4. Removing the duck breasts is done as follows: Place the bird breast side up. Remove any extra skin hanging from where the neck was. Also remove any collections of fat clinging to the rear cavity (all fat and trimmed skin can be placed in a small saucepan and melted down until just cracklings remain. The rendered fat is then strained and used for sautéing meats and fowl. It can also replace the oil in a salad dressing. The cracklings can serve as a garnish in a salad as well; see pages 160–61). Remove the wish-

bone under the remaining skin around the neck by cutting around it with the knife and pulling on it. With the duck still breast side up, cut along either side of the breastbone from the rear of the duck to the neck. Cut straight down to the bone. Using your fingers and the edge of the knife, peel the flesh away from the breastbone, little by little, until all the breast meat (including the little tenderloin strip that runs along each breast) is cut away from the body. Cut along the skin at the bottom of each breast to detach it completely. Place each breast skin side down and trim off the excess skin and fat.

5. Removing the duck legs is next: Turn the carcass onto one side with the breast toward you. Pull up on the leg and thigh and cut under them to the joint connecting the thigh to the body. Pull the leg and thigh farther away to expose this joint. Cut through the joint and lift the leg and thigh off the body. Do the same on the other side. Turn the pieces, skin side down, and trim off any excess fat and skin.

6. You should have 4 pieces of usable duck: 2 breasts, each having a drummette attached; and 2 pieces of leg and thigh. When using duck, the leg and thigh are usually left attached to each other.

$\mathcal{M}$arinated Salmon (Gravlax)

Two 1-pound salmon fillets, skin on and all bones removed
1 tablespoon white peppercorns
2 tablespoons kosher salt or sea salt
2 tablespoons sugar
2 cups fresh dill, including stems, or fresh tarragon

1. Wash the salmon under cold running water. Dry well. Remove any pinbones left in the flesh with a tweezers.

2. Using the bottom of a skillet, crush the peppercorns. Combine them in a small bowl with the salt and sugar. Set aside.

3. Crush the dill stems with a mallet or the bottom of a skillet. This will release their flavor. Reserve.

4. Sprinkle one-third of the salt mixture in the bottom of a shallow glass or ceramic dish. Lay 1 fillet in the dish, skin side down. Sprinkle with half the remaining salt mixture and cover with all the dill. Salt the second fillet on both sides with the rest of the mixture and place on top of the first, skin side up. Place a small plate on the salmon to weight it down slightly. Cover with plastic wrap and refrigerate for 3 days. Each day, remove the top piece and baste both fillets with the juices forming in the bottom of the dish. Replace 1 piece on top of the other, cover, and refrigerate again.

5. After 3 days, scrape off the dill and the salt mixture. To serve, slice on an angle to the cutting surface, but not through the skin. The slices should be as thin as possible, not more than ⅛-inch thick.

NOTE If you are planning to serve the salmon with a vinaigrette, refrigerate the liquid that has formed in the dish. Strain it and add some to the dressing for increased flavor.

Small Artichokes

Small artichokes vary in length from 1 to 2 inches. Fortunately, the inedible thistlelike choke found in large ones is not yet developed in the smaller varieties. They weigh about 1⅓ ounces each, 12 to a pound. You may as well cook a pound or two at a time, since you'll find they are quite versatile.

¼ cup freshly squeezed lemon juice
1 pound small artichokes (approximately 12)
1 teaspoon salt
1 bay leaf
2 cloves garlic unpeeled, pierced with the tines of a fork

1. Combine 1 quart water and the lemon juice in a mixing bowl.

2. Work with 1 artichoke at a time. Tear off the coarser outer leaves until you reach the yellowish softer ones. Using a chef's knife, cut off the top quarter of the artichokes, as well as the stem. Using a paring knife or swivel-bladed vegetable peeler, remove the tough dark green skin around the base. Place each trimmed artichoke in the acidulated water as you finish trimming it.

3. When the artichokes are prepared, transfer them, along with the acidulated water, to a stainless-steel saucepan. Add the salt, bay leaf, and garlic. Bring to a boil, reduce heat to a simmer, and cook for approximately 10 to 12 minutes, until tender in the center. Do not cook them so long that they begin to fall apart.

4. When done, let the artichokes cool in the cooking liquid. When they reach room temperature, they can be refrigerated in the same liquid for up to 3 days; or they can be drained, quartered lengthwise, and marinated with herbs, olive oil, and lemon juice.

INDEX